Extremely convicting. Takes a wife and mother's position to a place where God wants it to be. Reveals His perfect design and blessing as a result.

Betty Martin
Wife, mother and teacher

As I read this book, my heart was touched by the knowledge of my place as a woman. I was thrilled to find this well-written and easy-to-read book. Of the many "virtuous woman" books written, this by far is truly a woman's handbook.

Shirley Harkins
Legal Secretary

As a single, self-employed woman, this book is a business asset. A correct understanding of submission enabled me to provide the kind of service that wins favor even in a competitive market.

Lee Andrews
Interpreter

I followed in my very independent mother's footsteps. As a single parent, I raised my daughter the way my mother raised me. Reading this book, I was relieved to begin to understand my role as a woman of God in the way that Jesus had intended it to be. I'm excited for my teenaged daughter to read this book in hopes that she will not get her role crossed with anything other than what God intended her to be. I am very excited about the new "me."

Nancy Butterfield
Nurse

A corporate wife with a teenaged son, I have followed my husband through three international moves. I thank God for the clear and practical guidance in this book which I need for my role and purpose as a woman in my home.

Ginny Stinson
Wife and mother

Several months since reading Mary Jean's book, a deep sense of encouragement remains. What great assurance to know that practicing Scriptural principles in my home, in my relationships and in my work with young people will in time profit all concerned. Mary Jean allowed me to catch a glimpse of the beautiful mosaic which is God's master plan for those I touch, created by seeming unconnected applications of the Word of God.

Ruth Vesely
Wife, mother, bookkeeper, youth director

We've Come a Long Way, Baby!

So Where Do We Go From Here?

We've Come a Long Way, Baby!

So Where Do We Go From Here?

by
Mary Jean Pidgeon
with J.C. Webster

Tulsa, Oklahoma

Unless otherwise indicated, all Scripture quotations are taken from the *King James Version* of the Bible.

We've Come a Long Way, Baby!
So Where Do We Go From Here?
ISBN 0-89274-725-0
Copyright © 1994 by Mary Jean Pidgeon
Mary Jean Pidgeon
Restoration of Women's Virtues
P.O. Box 440754
Houston, Texas 77244-0754

Published by Harrison House
P. O. Box 35035
Tulsa, Oklahoma 74153

Dedicated to:

My patient and loving husband, Jack, without whom I would not have had the courage to grow, and to Michael, Jack and Troy.

Special Thanks to:

Lynne Pearson, Joyce Dowell and Lois Griswold for their participation and support in getting this book finished. And to Marti Clark whose comments and criticisms helped clarify my thoughts.

And a great big loving thanks to Michael, Jack and Troy, whose stories pepper this book in the same way they have seasoned my life. Without your dad, I wouldn't have had the courage to grow, and without you three, I would have missed out on much of my growth. Thank you for being you. I love you!

Contents

Introduction

My search for truth about womanhood started when I first met Jesus Christ and began my search to discover my rightful place in His organization of the universe. After all, how can Jesus live His apparently masculine life through a female? Reading the Bible with its stories of great men of God puzzled me. With this wealth of information to guide them, the men seemed to have a clear-cut blueprint for life. But the precise role of the woman seemed to be a muddle over which many Christians haggled. This controversy still rages today. An army of voices shout messages to women varying from "You're worth whatever you want" to "Keep silent!" There is a God-ordained balance between these two extremes, but as a new Christian I felt stuck somewhere between them, not knowing exactly where that balance lay. Desperately wanting to know the truth and to do the right thing, I cried out to the Lord, and He began to reveal to me His answer — an answer which grew and solidified over a period of years and continues to enlarge itself in scope and clarity today.

Along the way I learned the word "virtue" whose synonyms include courage, strength, conformity, moral excellence and chastity, among others. After many years I felt that God had called me to help women restore their virtue, their strength. As I began teaching others, the belief grew stronger that the restoration of women's virtues is part of God's overall restoration movement in His Church today. God has allowed me to be part of that movement, teaching women both in the United States and overseas. The Lord is sovereignly ushering in a fresh revelation of woman's God-ordained submission without making her a doormat, and woman's God-given power without making her a monster. The work of the Church in these last days depends in great measure on this new awakening of woman's purpose, position and power.

My life's history was like that of so many other women today — whether married, divorced, re-married, a single working mother, a stepmother, a new Christian or the wife of a non-Christian. My history changed, however, when I began my earnest search for and careful application of God's plan and role for me as a woman. The Lord guided me through the mine fields of contradictory teachings to truly inspired books, tapes, teachers and ministers who enlarged my understanding of His Word and greatly stabilized me in my womanhood. As I carefully studied and applied the truths that God revealed, my life and the lives of many around me changed. I use personal examples throughout this book not to flaunt my own experiences, but to offer hope by way of example that good can result even from bad once we commit to live by God's plan. Today my husband is a pastor, my grown children are Bible-believing Christians and I am blessed beyond my greatest dreams.

Unfulfilled women today are crying out as I was — often from a position of neglect, from a heart of bitterness and a sense of reproach that has come down through the centuries to our generation. Much of secular society seems to consider the Church the last place to look for the answers to life's most difficult issues, yet we Christians have *the* Answer, Jesus Christ. It is only in Him that all people — male and female — discover their true purpose, position and power.

Do women have power? Yes! When we understand

the purpose for which woman was uniquely created, and position ourselves to fulfill that purpose, we will see power released — life-changing power, power over circumstances, power to live, power in the realm beyond our senses, immeasurable power, the power of the omnipotent Creator God.

My aim in this book is to lay out the truths of God's Word and to encourage you to follow God's design for womankind. My prayer is that the Lord will give you spiritual wisdom and understanding as you read, that His Holy Spirit will minister to you and that your virtues will be restored so that you may find completion and fulfillment as a woman in Christ.

Chapter 1

Woman's Unique Purpose

We've come a long way in our womanhood, yet the opening lines in this *USA Today* newspaper article by Karen S. Petersen sound surprisingly familiar:

> "'Why can't you ever come to the point?' he asks. Her circumlocutions drive him crazy.
>
> "'Why won't you really talk to me?' she asks. His silence makes her back arch."

In spite of our efforts to prove woman's equality, it appears we have neither understood our true uniqueness nor embraced our differences from men.

After all our advancement, we are still frustrated when the men don't talk and the women are accused of talking too much. Men tend to see the visible; women sense the invisible. Women hear nuances of speech and feel slight changes in relationships. Men focus on physical surroundings, goals, productivity and hobbies. Women feel frustrated with men for their lack of understanding, their refusal to communicate. Men are frustrated with women for changing their minds and nagging. As communication degenerates, men generally make accusations, women issue ultimatums. Everyone loses.

So where do we go from here?

The make-up of each of the sexes was created by God

to enable men and women to complement each other in the most stable, permanent bond in human society. A woman's unique make-up equips her for special purposes in all other areas of her life as well. Yet today many women feel unfulfilled, oppressed, alone and powerless.

How did we drift so far from our original purpose? More importantly, how can we change our course, especially if another person is involved? The answers require digging.

Much of the stress we women feel today results from not understanding our purpose, or from understanding only someone else's purpose for us. We may try to make our lives fit other people's expectations or fulfill other people's philosophies, yet we will remain unfulfilled if the innate, God-given goals for our lives remain unmet. When we don't know our purpose, it is impossible to become satisfied in achieving it. When we learn our purpose, we can get into position spiritually and physically to release power through our lives to accomplish that purpose.

Once in a correct position, we allow God's power to flow through us, influence without controlling, speak wisdom without overwhelming with words, exercise power without stifling ego, and act on sensitive impulses without charging in wrong directions.

I learned much about all this the hard way.

My husband, Jack, and I accumulated three sons in a yours-mine-and-ours marriage, all three of whom I will call "Charlie" in this book. I am proud of them all now, but back when they were growing up, especially in their teens, and while Jack and I were still working out our relationship, there were some trying times. It really doesn't matter who did what, only that we all survived, successfully even, and

God used my family to teach me a thing or two. The boys are all on their own now and the family times when we come back together are filled with laughter and jokes about those horrible "good ole days."

"Mom, I taught you everything you know," Charlie loves to say. In a way, he did.

As I struggled to find my place in life, raising three boys challenged my feminine sensibilities and strained my mental functions. I had to stretch to grasp what they might be thinking or doing at any given moment. That was when I first learned for certain that men and women are different. I had to struggle to understand their boyish minds that were so alien to memories of my mild girlhood. I was often ready for someone to provide me with a way out of the whole mess. I remember once going to a respected friend for help.

"Carl," I said, "listen to what Charlie is doing." I listed several aberrant behaviors from scorching furniture with a wood-burning set to out and out rebellion. I had become so concerned about the constant turmoil that I thought Jack and I had either sociopaths or absent-minded geniuses on our hands.

"Is this normal?" I asked after my discourse.

Carl looked at me with a caring pastoral expression and quietly said, "Yes, Mary Jean, these behaviors are normal for boys that age."

Both my greatest hopes and worst fears were realized in Carl's few words. On the one hand, I was happy to know that my children were normal. On the other hand, I was frightened to learn that there were no special schools or hospitals that offered a cure. Oh Lord, I was going to have to live with this and raise them myself!

Even worse than the struggles with my family were the struggles within myself. Insecurities, fears, lack of self-confidence, feelings of low self-esteem, all kept me frustrated much of the time. When I stretched to the limits of my own abilities, I finally realized that I needed greater power than what was within myself humanly so I called out to God for help and He heard me.

As I look back now to those early years after my conversion to Christianity, I can see where my family became my University of the Word. My kitchen table became my desk, the Bible became my resource book, my children were ongoing assignments and Jack was an associate professor whom I thought graded too hard. Through the difficult tests and successes in this school, God taught me who I was as a person and as a woman, and I grew enormously, both internally and in outward relationships.

God showed me that His purpose for my life included more than my being simply "a wife and mom," which generally means mastery as cook, tutor, lover, nurse, secretary, bookkeeper, chauffeur and so forth. There was more to being "me" than such externals. God gave me His perspective so I could understand the real world around me and my true purpose in it. I couldn't perceive it on my own. God's worldwide, ageless perspective and omniscience allows Him to see where each of us is, as well as where He intends us to be. God gives us the power to fulfill our purpose, so it is important to become focused on Him and His purpose for us, whether we are raising children, working, adjusting to widowhood, getting married or just barely hanging on. Knowing the purpose of being must come before exercising the power of achieving.

God never produces anything without a purpose. Our unique purpose as women is the basis for everything we do every minute of every day. It does little good for a marooned sailor to find a radio if he has no idea what it is for or how to use it. We may feel marooned ourselves and without the necessary tools for successful living, yet God has given us everything we need if we will only learn His purpose for us.

The word "purpose" refers to an intention, a determination, an end to be attained. God's purpose for us is His intention for our lives, what He has determined for us and the end to be attained by our living.

Before we were formed in our mother's wombs, you and I were given purpose.[1] God knew His plan for us before birth. We were not a random product of two people who may have had sex casually. We were thought of by God long before our biological parents ever dreamed of bringing us into this world. Even my children were formed in this way, although each from different circumstances.

Mankind has created things and not been sure of their use. The story of the invention of "Post-It" notes, or "stickies," is now a part of modern American folklore. A secretary reportedly asked an engineer at her company to create a special glue so she could attach notes to a page and later remove them. When the engineer returned with his creation, it worked so well that other office members began to demand a supply. The adhesive was marketed on yellow paper squares and became an overnight sensation, then an office necessity.

Man creates, not knowing the outcome. But God always knows the purpose and the end result of His creations. There is nothing haphazard or random with God.

Einstein motivated his students to search things out by proclaiming, "God didn't play dice with the universe."[2] Unless we search out God's purpose for our lives we will never discover it. We must come to a place where just living, or letting life happen to us, is less desirable than spending the time with God in prayer and study of His Word — to *learn*.

I spent a good part of my early years in a vague state of mind. I knew there was something more to life, yet I was content to rock along day after day without putting myself to the trouble to find out what it was. Finally, out of frustration with what was happening, and *not* happening in my life, I cried out to God for help. He answered my cry in a most exciting way, and the excitement has only increased through the years. As the Bible tells us, He is "no respecter of persons"[3] and will answer in an equally exciting way anyone who honestly seeks Him.

One day after I gave my life to Jesus, I had a unique experience as He began to thaw out my frozen existence. I was in my car running errands and singing along to a popular song on the radio when the words suddenly became clear about the wonderful places to which this songwriter had traveled and the great things she had done. Without thinking, I began to complain out loud about how boring my life was by comparison. Suddenly my heart seemed to hear the Lord say that this woman was "eating her seed."

"Eating her seed!" I said, "What on earth does that mean?"

The meaning suddenly sprang into my consciousness: God gives life as a seed, and this woman was eating it instead of planting it. Scriptures began to flood my mind that unless a seed dies and is buried, it cannot begin to grow.[4] The Lord was communicating within my spirit to let me know that I had to die to my own desires and plant myself where He directed. It seems silly that God could speak to me in an instant of time while I was doing mundane errands, but now I know that He uses any opportunity to teach us, so great is His love and concern for us. That's where life with Him takes on its exciting edge. From that day forward I knew that God had a unique plan for me, a plan whereby He would lead me to plant my life to make it amount to something greater than myself and become truly meaningful. This is a wonderful truth.

Each one of us is unique. We are made up of three integral parts: the spirit, the soul and the body[5] In each part, we are different from everyone else, uniquely ourselves. In our uniqueness, we have a specific purpose and, in our own way, our purpose is vital. Nothing is wasted. No one is unimportant. No one is "just like all the others." None of us is an "extra" on the "set" of life.

My friend's great-aunt Gladys recently died at the age of one hundred. This woman lived in obscurity and died in the back bedroom of a great-grandchild's house. But as a young woman she had left home and given her heart to Jesus Christ. Through tear-stained letters, Gladys convinced her sisters also to put their faith in Him. One of those sisters had a son whom God called to preach. He didn't easily give his life to Jesus, but Gladys and her sisters prayed fervently for him, and as an adult he gave in to God. When he finally began to minister, he did it with all his heart. He has since entered his fifth decade of effective ministry and has brought thousands of people to the Lord.

An old, decrepit, age-blinded woman named Gladys left this world in obscurity, but entered heaven as a heralded saint of God. Where only a handful of people on earth knew her, there may have been hundreds — even thousands — who greeted her on the "other shore" who had benefitted from her prayers in a way that secured their eternal destiny. Although to this world her existence may have seemed obscure, there is no such thing as obscurity in God's eyes!

We don't know how our lives will affect eternity, but God does. This is a great revelation to grasp because our society has devalued human life so that people feel hopeless and worthless. Many, especially women, have lost their individuality as well as their value.

Once we accept that we are here on this earth for a specific purpose, it logically follows that we must search out that purpose. This requires discipline. Not everyone finds this "high" road, but God promises that everyone who seeks it with his or her whole heart will find it.[6]

The first thing I discovered in my search for purpose is the fundamental understanding of the spirit realm. We live in two different worlds simultaneously, the natural world and the spiritual world. If we choose to acknowledge only the natural world, then we leave out half of our total existence. And the half we are leaving out is the most important half because the natural world is built from the spiritual world.

In other words, *the world we see is made from the world we don't see.*[7]

Once we give our lives to Jesus, and He opens our spiritual eyes, we can see this world that has been around us all along.[8]

Within the spirit world are two realms or kingdoms. One is a kingdom of darkness which is ruled by Satan, a fallen angel who was cast out of the Kingdom of God.[9] The other is the Kingdom of Light[10] ruled by God through His

Son, Jesus Christ, with the power of His Holy Spirit.

Satan counterfeits every good thing God creates in an attempt to make us stumble into his kingdom. He deceives to make his counterfeits appear to be the genuine article. His kingdom has within it envy, strife, selfish ambition, confusion and every evil thing.[11] There is no unity, commitment, boundaries or discipline, only lawlessness and disobedience. Every person is free to do whatever he or she decides is right. There are no absolutes, no rights or wrongs. On the surface, this sounds great, but as a result of people adhering to this kingdom's lawless selfishness, we find ourselves in a society that is violent and often out of control.

Natural man, as a part of this kingdom, is an insatiable animal.[12] Sexual deviations and our depleted environment both testify to the insatiability of mankind. Without Jesus Christ in our lives we have no choice but to express the characteristics of the kingdom of darkness.

Jesus is the "light of the world."[13] God has committed Himself to us through His Son, Jesus Christ[14] and wants us to commit ourselves back to Him by obeying His Word.[15] In His Kingdom, there is commitment, unity, peace and love. We will find the purpose for His wonderful gift of life and the power with which He fills us the moment we believe in His Son Jesus.

The Kingdom of Light is not in any organization that calls itself "a church," but it is found in "the Church," meaning the entire body of believers who exalt Jesus, the Son of God Who shed His blood to forgive the sins of all people everywhere.[16] The Word of God is honored by the Church through obedience, commitment and sacrificial love. I once was part of a church, but not the Church. Being part of a church means remembering to set an alarm

Sunday morning in order to make it to a meeting on time and perhaps even shaking the minister's hand after the service or mass. Becoming part of the Church means conforming to the Will of God as He reveals it in His Word.

Within God's Kingdom is discipline. Like many women, I hopped on the bandwagon a few years ago and did the whole "get-in-shape" workout thing. My body may not remember it, but my mind held on to this one thing the exercise leader said, that disciplining our bodies gives us freedom. Although she may not have known it, this is a principle from God's Kingdom. There truly is a freedom in discipline because discipline liberates us from self-defeating sins, behaviors or habits. Discipline brings freedom.

In raising our sons, Jack and I realized that not only did we need to set boundaries and establish order, but that the disciplines we imposed made our sons more secure than if they grew up on their own. Children left to themselves, without rules or regulations, become insecure. People with some kind of guidance or direction feel secure. The disciplines of God's Word produce not only freedom but also a great sense of security in life.

Charlie tested and retested our discipline, but by remaining firm and consistent, Jack and I finally instilled in him the security that comes from knowing that someone is in charge. As a child of divorce, this was a very important step for Charlie. We have seen the fruit of it by seeing him develop into a mature, responsible adult who respects authority.

But discipline, by and large, is not easy for humans. In my own life, I put off disciplining my eating habits for a long, long time. When I finally brought them under the control of the Holy Spirit within me, the discipline set me free from a mind weighed down with thoughts and decisions about food. I was finally free to use my mind for much more productive pursuits.

Disciplines are not to be feared, but embraced. The idea of discipline is made far easier when we realize that it is God's grace that does the disciplining within us. His grace influences our hearts[17] and, when we cooperate with it, the result is discipline. Discipline to abide by God's purpose for us as women is not confining, but freeing because we can be completely ourselves and totally secure. When we put our trust in the stable, immovable anchor of Jesus Christ, fears and insecurities begin to wash away. When we find and adhere to His purpose for us, we are released to be our own unique selves, and to become fulfilled in all our inner longings.

The "do-your-own-thing" philosophy has sometimes created bondage in women's lives because the lack of discipline leads to a narrower, not broader, existence.

When an acquaintance named Kelly remarried she explained to a mutual friend that marriage gave her more freedom rather than less. Whereas in her first marriage she felt a sense of bondage from the boundaries placed around her, after divorcing she realized that she felt greater bondage without a husband because she had no one to help with her responsibilities, no one to talk to and no one with whom she could share. She found the small price of boundaries worth the sacrifice for the benefits of relationship.

My point is not that all women need to be married, but that boundaries are often not the drudgery they might appear to be. Resisting disciplines and boundaries leads us down a merry path to ultimate destruction.

Even love has disciplines. The Bible says that love does

25

not act "unbecomingly."[18] This actually means that love does not "lose its shape." Love has a form, a shape with boundaries. Without boundaries, love cannot exist. The Bible says that love never fails,[19] which makes it an important avenue of power. We can be sure of true love, and sure of love's boundaries.

Women are doing many things today, but only a few things are important and only one thing in life is absolutely necessary. The one essential thing is to enter into a love relationship with God in which we worship Him and focus on His will for our lives. So many miss their purpose for frivolous reasons. Pride in "doing our own thing" is not worth living below the level on which God intended for us to live. In a day of so-called freedoms, God is looking for women who will freely choose to do His Will. As He says, "This day . . . I have set before you life and death, blessings and curses. Now choose life, that you and your children may live."[20] If we choose life, we choose God's way. If we allow ourselves to be disciplined by His grace, we can achieve our unique purpose.

I can remember the day I truly met Jesus. I had attended church all my life and had responded as well as I could to what I knew about God, but I had never really been "born again."[21] I didn't realize that when a person is born again, Jesus gives that individual a new heart and a brand new beginning. Then one day I became tired of the grind, of weathering the storms for a reason I wasn't even sure of, and so I asked Jesus to come into my life and give me the power I needed to live my life as *He* desired. It was terribly simple, but I can honestly say that from that point on my testimony became, "Once I was blind but now I can see."[22] Though I had believed in Jesus for a long time, I had never verbalized my belief nor, until that moment, had I ever asked Him to become Lord of my life.[23] Once I did, I became awake to the spiritual world about me and entered into a relationship with Jesus that has truly changed me and my family.

Once we pass from the kingdom of darkness into the Kingdom of Light, God's enemy Satan becomes our enemy. Satan's desire and goal is to make us miss God's purpose and be on his side in his rebellion against God. When we choose to serve God, our lives become a glory to Him, which makes Satan furious, but he has no power over us.

When things are out of order in our lives, outside of the boundaries of love and God's Word, Satan can thwart our purpose, destroy our lives and steal God's glory. If this is happening to you, Jesus wants to help you. If you will ask Him to forgive you for any misunderstanding you have had in the past and for your sins, He will cleanse you of all your sins, come into your life and help you discover your purpose.

- Each of us has a specific purpose to fulfill on this earth and our purpose is vital.

- We need the power of God in our lives.

- There is no such thing as obscurity in God's eyes.

- The world we see is made from the world we do not see.

- The disciplines of God's Word produce great security in life.

- Love has boundaries; love never fails.

- Women are doing many things today, but only a few things are important and only one thing is absolutely necessary: to enter into a love relationship with God.

- Pride in "doing our own thing" is not worth living below the level on which God intended for us to live.

- Let Jesus into your life and you will discover your divine purpose.

Chapter 2

Woman Made in the Image of God

On a crisp winter morning I bundled my sons into jackets and drove them off to school. Blowing back into my house with a gust of wind, I closed the chilly weather behind me, grabbed a cup of coffee and headed for my next scheduled stop — the kitchen table where my Bible lay open and waiting for me. What a joy it was that all three boys finally left at the same time. As a young Christian, I was full of questions and now I could spend as much time as I needed to search through the Scriptures for answers. Instinctively I knew this was just a season of life, and I relished every moment I had alone with God.

That morning I decided to start all over again, beginning to read from page one of my Bible, starting with the Creation story. I read carefully down the first column, concentrating on every word, until I came across the line, "God created man in His own image, in the image of God He created him; male and female He created them."[1] Though the passage was familiar, it dawned on me that, as a woman, I was created in the image of God.

"Lord," I paused to ask aloud, "what part of me is like You?"

With unlimited patience, God began to teach me, and continues to teach me, the things I lay out here. Doing a word study, I discovered that the word "man" is translated from two different terms in the original language. One word means man as the male of the species, and the other means man-faced, or human. So the biblical term "man" often refers to mankind or humanity. Sometimes it refers exclusively to men, but the rest of the time we women are included, and we must be careful to interpret such references correctly.

God made "man," both male and female, in His image and gave them rule over His creation. As creatures of God, we were made for relationship with Him. So our first priority, which we've already discussed, is in developing our intimate love relationship with God.

But then God separated man into male and female. In so doing, besides changing their anatomy, He separated their purposes. Of the two types of God's power given to mankind in creation, one is the power of authority, and the other is the power of influence. The power of authority makes the decisions and the power of influence helps make and carry out those decisions. The functions of these two powers can be seen in any individual alone, but they tend to predominate in one sex or the other to help achieve their specific purpose. In other words, each of us can or will exercise all types of power at various times in our lives, even various times of the day. In relating to the male role, we will respond with the power predominating in the female, and vice versa. There is no inferiority on either part insinuated in God's perfect creation. All things are equal, fair and balanced. Yet to fulfill the different purposes, the two sexes exercise power differently.

Perhaps you have heard the short version of the creation of the world. First the Lord created plants. He looked at what He had made and said, "I can do better," so He created animals. Then He said, "I can even do better," so He created man. Then He said, "I can still do better," so He created woman. Then He said, "I can do no better," and rested. This is amusing, but wrong! We females were included in that first creation of man, the human being, who was made in God's own image.

"Man," the human being, was alone when God created him. After God made all the rest of creation, and said that it was "good," He looked at man and said that it was "not good" for him to be alone.[2] God was pleased with all the rest of creation, but with the human being created in His own image, He was not pleased.

I believe that God was displeased to have both the powers of authority and influence predominating within one creature. By separating the powers, God could express Himself more fully with a greater range of function in each. Whether or not this was His reason, the result was that God said He would make for man a "helper" or an aid. Woman is the helper He made. The word "helper" has far more meaning than the connotation given in the phrase "Mommy's little helper" because the kind of help God intended is derived from the image of God Himself.

The psalmist said that God is our Helper.[3] In the New Testament, Jesus said that He would send us a Helper.[4] This "helper" is the Holy Spirit Who serves as our Comforter, Intercessor, Counselor, Advocate and Helper.[5] When God separated man the human into man the male and female, He expected the female, created in His image, to help in a capacity similar to that of the Holy Spirit. *God expects woman to help as others' intercessor, counselor, advocate, comforter and helper.* This is the second important part of woman's purpose.

When God separated the female from the male, caus-

31

ing the two to walk side by side with separate purposes and powers, suddenly, the two needed each other. The male and female roles perfectly complete and complement each other. When the Bible talks about the Church as the Bride of Christ, we collectively in the Church are in the female role while Christ is in the male role. When Christ walked the earth, He subjected Himself to the authority of God the Father and in that sense put Himself into the female role. This is why we as women can become "Christlike" just as effectively as men. Jesus Christ is our example even though He manifested Himself as a male. No wonder the Apostle Paul was able to proclaim that in Christ "there is neither male nor female."[6]

In Scripture, primary roles and powers play a large part in the lives of men and women. God has obviously set out two primary positions, a dominant position for the male and an equally important helper position for the female. However, we operate in one role at one moment and in another the next. An executive may exercise authority when her daughter calls from home, then see her boss and exercise influence, then give instructions to her secretary and exercise authority again. This is obviously good and right. The single mom has a vacant position beside her which God fills with His love, and we will talk more about that later.[7] For the sake of clarity, we are separating these roles very distinctly, but we really fill different roles at different times.

Woman doesn't have the sole claim to operate as intercessor, counselor or comforter. Nehemiah filled the role of an intercessor,[8] the male prophets gave counsel, Paul the apostle comforted others.[9] Keep in mind the understanding that we can move in and out of male and female roles constantly.

The next interesting part of woman's purpose is in

relation to marriage. The Bible describes the wife as a "crown" to her husband.[10] When we see that the Lord Himself "crowns [us] with lovingkindness and compassion,"[11] we see how the woman again expresses the image of God. The verb form of the Hebrew word translated "crown" can mean "to *encircle* (for attack or protection)."[12] As a woman of God, one is to crown her husband, encompassing him about against attack and for protection, just as God does. I for one am guilty of having used my position to attack my husband, and I would guess that most wives would have to admit to the same fault. But the Lord never attacks. Instead, His crown is a protection of lovingkindness, compassion and favor against attack.[13]

As these things began to come clear to me, I reviewed my life and found that as crown, comforter, intercessor, counselor, advocate and helper, I lacked in all areas. Even though I knew that prayer was important, and prayed daily for each member of my family, I heard myself sounding more like a judge in my prayers than an intercessor. Neither my husband nor my sons, neither my pastor nor anyone else I knew, needed a judge. They needed an intercessor, someone who would "stand in the gap"[14] for them and plead for God's intervention in their lives.

A woman I will call Amy attended a Bible study I once taught. She was young, sweet and well-meaning, but frustrated about her marriage. The first day we took prayer requests, Amy glibly complained to us that her husband never listened to her. They had just lost money on a venture that she had warned him not to buy into, and he had done about a dozen other things all wrong. Later, when it came her turn to pray, almost her entire prayer was a complaint to God about her husband's failings and requests for Him to change her husband in specific ways. I felt bad for her because, however sincere, her prayer was largely one of judgment rather than love.

Later, I took Amy aside privately and learned the other half of the story. Once she prayed about something, she would habitually tell her husband everything he was supposed to do. No wonder he wasn't listening. She thought she found her purpose as his boss, not his helper. With some prayerful guidance, she made some fundamental changes, and her marriage dramatically improved.

If we try to make others change, thinking we are helping God, we misunderstand our role. God reserves for Himself the responsibility and power of changing people's hearts. We females so often try to usurp this power that we commonly joke about women trying to change men. On a recent television program I saw, a man tried to encourage a friend to continue in his relationship with a woman.

"Women see stuff in us that we can't see in ourselves," he said exuberantly. "They love us unconditionally . . . *Then* they try to change us!"[15]

He got a good laugh, because his words ring sadly true.

Instead of standing before God complaining to Him, we need to stand before the Throne of Grace as an advocate for those whom we have been assigned to help. The prayer greater than "Oh, God, change Brian" is "God, You Who are perfect and know every fault, please have mercy on Brian and move on his behalf by Your grace and out of Your great mercy and steadfast love."[16] See the difference?

The people in our lives, particularly our family members, are not random occurrences, but are assignments from God. These assignments are not reconstruction projects. In carrying out our assignment, we will learn, be tested, pass (or fail), and eventually graduate to greater and greater areas of responsibility and influence. The people we pray for may or may not change, but we definitely will be changed.

As for original man, it seems clear to me that he needed a helper. God's Word records that after he named all the animals, the Lord "caused a deep sleep to fall upon [him]."[17] When Adam fell asleep, the "womb of man," woman was brought out to help man's condition. Woman is also referred to as the "corresponding part"[18], one who would stand like him, but opposite him, and walk along beside him. As his inner, hidden chamber, she came out to be a physical reminder of the spirit realm. God emphasized His characteristics in her that involve heart, emotion, sensitivity and spiritual strength.

Eve was created uniquely by a "separate, creative act which has no parallel in history."[19] The way in which she was created and brought to the man gave him back more than the "womb" that had been taken from him.[20]

If creation were a contest, Adam and Eve tied.

If we take the word "rib" at face value, we come pretty close to what God did in separating the sexes. For example, the stiff parts of an umbrella that hold it up are the ribs. In a Houston downpour, I wouldn't want to stand under an umbrella without its ribs. On the other hand, I wouldn't want to stand under one with ribs only and no fabric. Both roles are equally important to achieve the desired outcome — in this case, not to get wet.

The woman was created to help the man become more in touch with the spirit realm, or the "hidden man of the heart."[21] But when woman came along, she became caught up in the things of the world and ate of the only forbidden tree, then influenced the man to do the same. I believe women are in this same state today, having been brought out to help a man reach greater righteousness yet stumbling over the same things he stumbles over and leading him deeper into sin. When we busy ourselves too much with the physical world, we neglect the spiritual.

In the Book of Hebrews, we are warned not to drift away from what we have learned.[22] It is easy to do. Since the matters of the heart are unseen to us, it takes longer to realize that we have drifted. When I let my yard or house go, I notice it pretty quickly. But when I become dull spiritually because of neglecting prayer and study of the Word of God, it takes awhile before the emptiness catches up with me. I used to wait until some huge calamity had struck before I would realize I had stopped praying. Now I know better. I have learned that I must discipline myself constantly to pay attention to the spirit realm.

The woman's power of influence is vital to the man, and the man's power of authority, which many people call a "covering," is vital to the woman.

If you have ever worked on a group project, from painting a mural in kindergarten to collaborating on launching the space shuttle, you have recognized the need for people to work together. Again, the roles we assume and the power we use change from situation to situation. Sometimes the role we play is a required one. When we are the engineer in charge of a project, it is important that everyone working for us follow our lead, whether male or female. When we leave the job and go to choir practice, others are in charge, and it is important for us to follow them, whether male or female. The issue is not in determining gender or function but in following the person to whom God has given the power of authority.

Other times the role we play depends on ourselves.

A woman friend of mine is horrified by the sight of a spider. If she saw a spider when a man was in the room, she would run shrieking and ask him to kill it. But if she were alone with her small children and saw a spider, she would rise to the occasion and kill it herself. She is exercising a different power each time, but getting the same end result. When a man is present, she exercises her power of influence to get him to kill the spider. When children are present, she operates with the power of authority to kill the spider herself.

The two powers could be characterized as the king and the priest or the Martha and Mary. Mary was a friend of Jesus' who sat at His feet listening to Him teach while her sister Martha busied herself in the kitchen preparing the meals.[23] We all have these two capacities within us, but we specialize in one or the other as we work with others on various projects. The king, or the Martha, sees to the decisions of the seen world, and maintains order through administration. The priest, or the Mary, is the visionary, creative thinker or meditator who sees to the unseen world and is an important influence in carrying out the decisions. We can be Marys in the morning, in worship and devotion to God, then Marthas just minutes later in dispensing orders for the day to the children or gardener.

Immediately following the separation of man into male and female, Adam and Eve came back together with a strong commitment to each other.[24] God intended to unite the sexes in covenant relationship as a perfect complement to each other in every way. Neither of them committed adultery, yet their covenant was broken when one of them made a decision independent of the other which ultimately led to their fall.

Centuries later, Paul wrote to Timothy that he did not allow the woman to "usurp authority" over the man.[25] The Greek word he used means "to *act of oneself*" or to be a "self-worker."[26] When Eve became a "self-worker," sin entered her covenant relationship with Adam. She was tempted by Satan, in the form of a serpent, to eat of the tree of the "knowledge of good and evil." Then Eve gave a fruit to her husband and he ate, too.[27]

I do not know of any theologians who blame Eve for Adam's actions. Wielding her power of influence, she encouraged her husband to eat, but Adam was responsible for his own decision and for the welfare of his household. Both shared the blame, and both rightfully shared the consequences of their sin.

Like Eve, many women seem to ruin their lives in similar ways. Eve lived a charmed life as the only daughter of God and the sole recipient of her husband's affection. I cannot help but wonder why she was so susceptible to the serpent's enticing words. Perhaps she was tired of waiting for Adam to make a move. Many of us are the same way; we get frustrated when the man in our life fails to catch on to what we sense is supposed to happen. Perhaps out of impatience, Eve acted independently, becoming a "self-worker" in order to force the man into action. It backfired on her, just as it does on impatient women today.

Or, perhaps Adam became overly involved in the physical realm and did not pay as much attention to his wife as she desired. Having been brought out from the man, a woman derives her feelings of self-worth largely from the men in her life, beginning with her father. If the male neglects to cherish and nourish the female, she can become vulnerable to Satan's lies. We see this scenario played out repeatedly in troubled girls who look for feelings of self-worth through self-defeating, often even illegal activities. And we see it with wives whose husbands spend more time with work or possessions than with them. These women will often leave their husband for another man, a social club, career or some other interest. Some women may even stay home and appear to be faithful but have overloaded themselves with "good works" to fill the lack in their lives.

Whatever Eve's reasons were, her story serves as a warning. If she could be that susceptible to Satan even while living in Paradise, how much more must we watch our hearts not to be drawn away and enticed.[28] If it is a sense of self-worth we need, God will give it to us freely and liberally. The really good news of the Gospel is that Jesus Christ fills in all the gaps. When we are not receiving the cherishing and nourishment we need, the Lord is there to provide it. He is a husband to the widow[29], a father to the fatherless[30], our best friend[31] and our greatest love.[32]

Jesus loves us and will supply all our need,[33] freeing us to be the person He created us to be. I am sure that men recognize needs in their lives that are unmet as well, and Jesus fills those, too. We are all learning to care for one another. Where we fail, Jesus fills in. Jesus never fails.

Whatever we learn about our purpose, we cannot escape the fact that woman was originally created to be in relationship with God, and was brought out of the man to correspond to him, be his helper, strengthen him and reveal to him the hidden matters of the heart. Although we live in an imperfect world that suffers the ravages of sin, the *ideal* is for the man primarily to carry the power of authority and the woman primarily to carry the power of influence. The woman's role accentuates the importance of her relationship with God. If she is to help others in the spiritual realm, she must herself be attuned.

- As women, you and I are made in God's image.

- Our first priority is in developing our intimate love relationship with God.

- The "power of authority" makes the decisions and the "power of influence" helps make and carry out those decisions.

- The female role is as counselor, advocate, intercessor, comforter and helper, and as the strength and crown.

- Women can become "Christlike" just as effectively as men.

- We move in and out of male and female roles constantly.

- Neither our husbands nor our children, neither our pastors nor anyone we know, needs a judge. They need an intercessor.

- Our role is to intercede and counsel, God's role is to change people's hearts.

- The people we pray for may or may not change, but we definitely will be changed.

- The woman's power of influence is vital to the man, and the man's power of authority, which many people call a "covering," is vital to the woman.

- Jesus fills in all the gaps.

Chapter 3

Unequalled Abilities

Three men picked up a lamp they found lying in the sand, rubbed it, and out popped a genie.

"For releasing me from my prison, I will give each of you one wish," the genie told them.

"I wish I could be ten times smarter," said the first man.

"You have your wish," answered the genie.

When the second man saw that the first had succeeded and prospered, he decided he would try his hand at this wishing game.

"I wish I could be a hundred times smarter," he said.

"You have your wish," the genie replied.

When the third man saw that the second man had done even better than the first in a short period of time, he determined to top them both.

"I wish I could be a thousand times smarter," he declared.

"You have your wish," the genie responded. "You are now a woman."

As silly this story is, it points out what all females know, that women have strengths and abilities that men simply do not have. Instead of recognizing their strengths,

41

many times over the years women have been scorned and made to be almost ashamed of their sex. I remember at every family gathering a family acquaintance would delight in putting down the women present, as if he took pleasure in spoiling the event for us females.

Encountering a person who tries to make women feel inferior is part of every female's experience. For some women this may happen once, for others it is an ongoing campaign they must deal with daily. The inequality of the sexes is actually a borrowed philosophy from the ancient Greeks, having nothing to do with Christianity. Yet Christians have been accused of perpetrating the myth and Holy Scripture has been perverted.

The truth is that both male and female are dependent upon each other and can bring about God's perfect will when they work together, building up each other's strengths. The Bible says that just as "woman is *of* the man, even so is the man also *by* the woman; but all things [are] of God."[1] Again, there is a difference yet equality between them. Man is woman's point of origin because she is "of" him. She originates from the seed of man and was created for man. Being for the man, in a marriage relationship she submits herself and her power of influence to him and his power of authority.

The Apostle Paul said that God is the Head of Christ, Christ is the Head of the man and the man is the head of the woman.[2] This "headship" principle, though unpopular with many, is scriptural. However, the man is the "head" only of the woman with whom he has come into agreement in a marriage relationship. In that union, both individuals bring something specific to the other. The man is to bring headship, steadiness and security, and the woman is to bring discernment, influence and strength of heart, which are equally important, valuable and powerful.

To clear up an old misconception, the Bible does not say that all men are head over all women. Neither does the Bible say that all women must submit to all men. A specific man is the head of one specific woman who has agreed to submit to his headship through marriage.

The phrase "the man is by the woman" can also be translated "the man is through the woman." According to Strong's concordance, both these words denote "the *channel* of an act."[3] The man comes through the woman in his natural birth, and I believe he is greatly influenced by the woman in his spiritual birth as well. Being created from the inner "chamber" of the man, the woman wields a strong influence on his "hidden man of the heart." One of the reasons why God created man to be drawn to woman is so he would watch her[4] and be influenced by her heart. Because what a man sees exerts a tremendous impact upon him, he can be drawn into the woman's relationship with God without her even saying a word.[5]

The woman is part of, for, and originated in the man. The man is by and through the channel of the woman.

Translated into real life, this means that the Christ-centered wife who is growing spiritually, and giving attention, love and ministry to her husband, will find that her love and support for him greatly affects his inner spiritual growth. This is not to say that a husband turns out bad because his wife did not do enough! It is simply a challenge for women to become aware of their primary responsibility to God, so He can work through them in the lives of those around them.

I remember observing a friend named Phillip who met

and fell in love with a woman named Kindy late in his life. When they married, Kindy loved Phillip very deeply and demonstrated her love toward him in her very obvious care for him. He didn't demand much because he was simply so happy that he had found her, and she didn't act in an obsequious manner toward him, for after years of single living, she was completely her own woman. Nevertheless, she loved him thoroughly, openly and without reservation.

When her lavish love continued even after the "honeymoon was over," I began to note a change in Phillip. Everyone acquainted with the two began talking about it. Through Kindy's honor, love and respect for Phillip, he was quite obviously becoming more of a man, and more spiritually attuned to God. Before the marriage, he had expressed little interest in spiritual things, but now he was responding in ways we had never seen him do before.

Actually, the transformation convicted me as it pointed out weaknesses in my own life and some of the poor habits into which I had fallen. About that same time, God had been showing me the importance of the woman's influence on the man's life. As a woman surrounded by men, this display of love-in-action served as a divine sermon illustration to me.

The power of love cannot be overstated. Since the Bible is the source of all truth, and since it says clearly that "love never fails,"[6] we must realize that love is a pretty powerful attribute. This verse does not refer to emotional love, for that kind of "love" is weak and is bound to fail. The love that never fails is true, committed love. This is the kind of love that says, "I'm on your team, and one of the purposes of my existence is to see that you fulfill your potential in life." This is the kind of love God has for each of us. Because God fills us with such love, it is the kind of love husbands and wives, pastors and congregations, brothers and sisters can (and should!) manifest toward each other.

The Bible says that a wife is to respect and reverence her husband.⁷ God gave woman the capacity and desire to give this reverence and respect, and it is important for the man to receive it. Likewise, the man has been endowed with a love and protection which he needs to give,⁸ and the woman needs to receive.

Since Jesus Christ is sufficient to fill in all the gaps, if just one person in a given circumstance will begin to do his or her part, the whole situation can fall into place. Jesus has paid the ultimate price at the Cross to release into our lives His mighty resurrection power that causes even dead things to spring back to life. This is why one Bible teacher admonishes, "Don't pray for a renewed marriage; pray for a *resurrected* marriage!"⁹

The idea of a tremendous reservoir of spiritual power lying within the woman is a difficult concept for some to grasp. Many women have heard for years about "headship," and thought it was a teaching of inequality tilting toward male domination. Such people have missed the point that although the man is the head of the family, the woman carries a great deal of the power through influence. That's why athletes look at the camera and say "Hi, Mom!" They're not consciously belittling Dad, just intuitively recognizing Mom's influence and power in their accomplishments.¹⁰

When God separated the male and female and gave them different powers and manifestations of Himself, He also separated them biologically to enable each one to fulfill his or her specific purpose. Although we know that women have babies and men don't, other tremendous biological differences are only recently being uncovered by science, and creating quite a stir. Some feminists have minimized the differences between the sexes and complained of inequality in the home, on the job, in government and in the military. The truth is, men and women *are* different, and the difference is from birth, not just the result of environment. The proof now offered by science, even by female scientists, is a tough pill for some feminists to swallow. Responding to a book by British geneticist, Dr. Anne Moir, entitled *Brain Sex: The Real Difference Between Men & Women* (Lyle Stuart), anthropologist Helen Fisher said, "Her book is courageous. She says things Americans will not want to hear."[11]

Male and female were originally created when God separated the feminine attributes from the male, leaving him only the masculine attributes. This same phenomenon recurs within the womb every time a child is developed. When a baby is conceived, for three months he or she looks like a female. Remember the woman's X and man's Y chromosomes from your biology class? The developing child, the embryo, looks like a female whether it has an XX or XY combination. But by the sixth week an XY embryo calls for his mother's supply of male hormones (which every woman has, to a lesser degree than men). When these hormones rush into the developing child, sexual differentiation occurs in two areas — the genitalia and the brain.[12]

The fact that the male embryo passes through the female form before becoming male reemphasizes the scriptural principle that the woman originates in the man and the man develops through the woman.[13] Neither stands alone.

The difference that comes about in the baby's genitalia is rather well known and even celebrated, but the differentiation of the brain is surprising. The two hemispheres of the brain are connected by a communications network called the corpus callosum. When the boy baby calls for the mother's androgens, they saturate and permeate the male brain, greatly simplifying the corpus callosum and specializing functions of the left hemisphere that are not repeated in the right hemisphere.[14]

The net effect is that the male brain no longer communicates as freely between the two hemispheres and becomes more specialized. In the female brain the communications network remains intact and many functions are duplicated in both hemispheres.

To reduce this concept to the simplest of terms, the female brain has twice as much going on in it. The female communicates back and forth between two hemispheres, so compared to the male she has twice as much to understand and twice as much to say. Unfortunately, she also has twice as much potential for error. The male has a narrower view, but is generally not as easily swayed.

I know this explanation sounds technical, but we don't have to be brain surgeons to see that men and women are different! Any relationship with a man will provide a woman with proof, if she is open to accept it. Just think of a time you have tried to tell a man everything that's on your mind. He may have listened, but grown wearied or complained that you "talk too much." On the other hand, when women get together, they generally are energized by "talking it all out."

In a radio interview, I heard a doctor compare the female brain to a computer. Press the right button, he said, and out spews information. How the woman arrived at the information may be uncertain, because sometimes women simply "know" without being able to explain how. The male brain he compared to the old-fashioned adding machine. Punch in the information and pull down the handle. It takes longer to get an answer, but once you do, you will have the proof right there on the tape.[15] The woman may pick up things using her highly active sensors, her intuition, but the man will wait for the facts. Because of these differences, the woman may sometimes feel that the man is insensitive, slow, uninterested or unspiritual. The man may think of the woman as emotional, unstable, silly.

The first thing you may think of are all the exceptions to these distinctions. Men and women are born with natural abilities unique to the individual, as well as attributes that are unique to their sex. One of my sons loves to talk, yet he is completely male. Again, we are dividing things only to see them clearly, not because our world is black and white. In Christ, there is no male or female, yet in the flesh there is. So, when the flesh is put in order, subject to the Spirit, we flow freely in the Spirit and these things matter far less. But apart from perfect living, we need to understand these principles to enable us to understand the Lord and what He ultimately desires to accomplish in our lives.

Accepting the differences between the sexes actually frees us to utilize and explore our natural strengths. In *TIME* magazine's cover story, "Why Are Men and Women Different?" researchers who are uncovering distinctions between male and female brains predicted that "confirmation of innate differences in behavior could lead to an unprecedented understanding of the mind."[16] Accepting our differences frees us to greater exploration and discovery. The article concluded that "some misunderstandings between the sexes may have more to do with cross-wiring than cross-purposes."[17] This insight recalls Rhett Butler's fictional line to Scarlett O'Hara in *Gone With the Wind*, "It seems we've been at cross purposes, doesn't it?"[18]

Our differences have caused many a split between man and woman, but were actually placed within us to fulfill our specific, God-given purposes. If a man is to be in a place of leadership, as the "head" of his family, then it is good for his brain to be equipped with leadership qualities. And it is. He is generally able to judge and decide without as much distraction as a woman might experience.

A woman, on the other hand, has more language capability and capacity. The Bible says of the Lord and His people, "He sent his word, and healed them."[19] God's Word is powerful and, since we are created in His image, our words are also powerful. Words are spiritual containers. Because women have been given more language potential, they have access to more words, or more spiritual containers. Most people acknowledge "woman's intuition" even if they are unaware of the spiritual origin of it. Now researchers have attributed this ability to the woman's thicker corpus callosum, and have discovered that this sensitivity is what helps her decipher what a baby tries to communicate.[20] So the woman has more spiritual sensitivity, intuition and language capacity, all of which helps fulfill her God-given purposes.

The woman's brain comes into contact with more information but generally has greater difficulty making a decision with the information. Her brain continues bouncing pros and cons back and forth utilizing both hemispheres. This is why we women are often stereotyped as changing our minds as in the classic furniture scene: "No, move the couch against the other wall again and the piano back over there."

As the woman collects facts she can become confused. The barrage of information can even affect her emotionally. To cope, she will find someone with whom she can have a good, long talk. Usually by the time she has finished discussing the situation, she will have sorted out some of the information and will feel much better.

Generally speaking, the man would be worn out by her "good, long talk." He is predisposed to making decisions, but he doesn't come into contact with as much information. Without the full information the woman can provide, he may unwittingly make bad decisions. With his "specialized" brain and lesser communication capacity, he is not bothered by the awareness of information that inundates the woman. As a result, he is freer to become focused, but he is also subject to his own narrow world which his ego tends to rule.

So, speaking in generalities, women can become foolish, distracted, and overly talkative, but men can become lost in their own egos and a narrow view of life. The best thing for both of them is to come together as co-laborers,[21] just as God intended. Although it can be frustrating to work things out with someone who sees things so differently, still I wonder how we men and women got so confused about all of this situation, since our strengths correspond to and complement each other's so perfectly.

When I became aware of the different workings of my brain and the male brains around me (there were four of them, my husband's and three sons'), I became much more free in my expression as a female. In counseling women, I have learned that appreciating these differences is the antidote to many of their complaints. When I hear, "He doesn't talk to me enough," I know that if this woman will accept the differences that exist between her and the male in her life, and change her expectations, the result will help free the man and herself.

Taking the generalities into consideration, it is interesting to see how we can relate to the opposite sex on a daily basis. My son, who defies all known research by being a talker, is naturally understanding of women, but he also frustrates them because they can't get out as much language as they want to around him. My husband Jack, on the other hand, could be the poster child for male brain research.

Jack and I have a standing joke about his workday. Each evening when he comes home, I am always eager to hear the details of his work. When I ask how his day went he will always respond "good" or "very good." After he accepted Christ, then became out-and-out "fired up" for Jesus, he sold his business and joined the pastoral staff of a church. He would leave at seven-thirty in the morning, return at five-thirty that afternoon, have had interaction with people and projects that I cared deeply about throughout the course of his day. But all he would say when he got back home was "good" or "very good."

Then we read a book that pointed out, "Men are headliners and women are fine print people."[22] Once we both understood this principle, I began to get the details from Jack by asking him a series of questions.

"As soon as you walked into your office, who was the first person who called?"

"Who else did you talk to?"

"Who did you have lunch with?"

When Jack began to understand my need for information, this repartee became a kind of game with us, and he would slowly retrace his steps to give me the details in which I was so vitally interested.

Many men refuse to be drawn out in this way and feel that women are grilling them instead of showing interest in them. Before Jack and I developed our communication game, I learned I could get the information by inviting friends over whom Jack enjoyed. During the conversation I would discover all the information I wanted. This was not a time to leave the presence of our guests and angrily confront Jack with, "Why didn't you tell me first?" I understood that it had never even occurred to Jack to tell me, or that he simply didn't have the energy to get out the words to tell me, until he was in that comfortable setting with his friends.

I had to learn not to take things so personally. Men often don't know how to communicate their feelings. In addition, what seems important to us women does not always seem important to them. One of our jobs as a "helper" is prayerfully to assist our mate in learning how to share his heart. As a man shares his heart with another person, he gets in touch with himself. This is also true of the woman, of course. Drawing out a person requires the wisdom of God Who has promised us that He will give us wisdom freely if we will just ask for it.[23]

When the male and female work together, generally it is the woman who picks up on things in the spirit realm, senses the needs of others around them and shares that information with the man. Her wide perspective is channeled into his narrow view through her words. He is typically able to focus, sift the information and help identify the mind and will of God in any given situation. When men alone make decisions without someone fulfilling this vital female role, their focus can be too narrow. When women alone make decisions without someone filling the crucial male role, they may leave themselves open to be moved or influenced by superficial stimuli.

God's perfect will is brought about when men and women work together, respecting one another's strengths and weaknesses.

As we grow as individuals into the fullness of Christ, we will find that we develop both aspects of male and female qualities, because they are both within us. But as we come together, we fulfill our part depending on the role we play. In my ministry of "Restoration of Women's Virtues," I act in the male role as the leader, which is the proper exercise of the position God has given me. But when I come home to Jack, I function together with him in a female role. When Jack is in his private devotions with the Lord, he develops his inner man and becomes sensitive to the unseen world around him. But when we come together in unity, I carry much of this spiritual awareness. As we work together as husband and wife, the fullness of God is represented in us.

So how do we get to this point of mutual cooperation? Primarily through knowledge, respect, the grace of God and attitude control!

As I was growing up, there was no male role model in the family. On my father's rare visits home he was deeply involved in business. His outlet was alcohol, which brought him to an early death. As a result of this void, I never learned to respect a male. When I began as a teenager to develop relationships with men, they were unhealthy ones that led to further loss of respect toward all males in general and eventually a painful divorce. God had to heal me in this area of my life and correct my wrong attitudes. In order to allow God's healing, I had to discipline myself to accept His correction and learn to respect the male as a human being created in the image of God, but made differently from me. As I surrendered my old hurts, God taught me respect.

When this transformation began, I was married to Jack and doing volunteer work at Charlie's school. One day as I sat doing some mindless task, I casually looked out the office window and saw a man in the hall. He was waiting for someone, standing straight and tall, his suit well tailored and hanging beautifully down to his highly polished shoes. A feeling came over me that puzzled me at first. I knew I was not attracted to this man, but I may have blushed as I looked back down. My mind raced to pinpoint what I was experiencing. I looked back and saw that he was still there, in all his societal trappings of manliness. Suddenly I realized what I felt. It was respect! This event was a turning point for me. I found that I respected the manly image of this total stranger.

In that experience, Jesus was teaching me to appreciate His own manhood.

After God had healed me quite a bit, Jack and I started working in the singles department of our church. I remember seeing many young women enter our group with cold hearts. They were beaten up by circumstances and hardened in their attitudes. Many of them denied any need of a man, had no desire to marry and certainly did not want children if they did marry. As they would receive Jesus Christ into their lives, and allow the Word of God to mature them spiritually, they would grow and change. Without fail, they would relent. First they would admit that perhaps one day they would marry if God really wanted them to, then they would accept the idea of having children. With all the wedding and baby gifts we purchased, Jack and I could have bought a new car! God is the great Healer and Equalizer, and it was our joy to see these precious people healed and matured in Him.

Of course, there were those who never married, but of those who truly followed Jesus, none of them abstained from marriage because of disrespect, a bad attitude or an unyielding heart. I am certainly not claiming that women must marry and bear children in order to fulfill their divine purpose in life. I am claiming, however, that when we are truly yielded to Jesus Christ, He always replaces the world's coldness and Satan's lies with natural desires and godly attitudes.

I know this hardened attitude toward men is not uncommon among women today. I encourage you to take inventory of your own attitudes. It may be that men have let you down through the years, and you are angry. I believe a lot of women today are mad at men for wounds of the past, and justifiably so, by the world's standards. This is where Jesus makes a difference in life that nothing else and no one else can, because He not only commands us to change, He also enables us to change. No one and no program can change a heart, but He can.

If you have anger or resentment in your heart toward men in general or a certain man in particular, first, to be truly healed you must realize your anger and take responsibility for it. After all, no one can "make" you mad. "Mad" is what you have selected from an array of choices. And it is truly the wrong choice, for we don't hurt anyone but ourselves when we harbor anger. Then, you must repent of your attitude before God. Next you must be willing to forgive, as an act of obedience, even though emotionally you are not ready or able to do so. Finally, you must continue every day releasing, repenting and forgiving, until God has completely replaced your bitter, negative attitude with His loving, positive attitude.

Male and female are born to complete each other and reflect the image of a holy and powerful God. And we are just beginning to uncover the good part!

- The woman is part of, for and originates in the man. The man is by and through the channel of the woman.

- The woman's love and support for the man greatly affects his inner spiritual growth.

- Since Jesus Christ is sufficient to fill in all the gaps, if just one person will begin to do his or her part, the whole situation can fall into place.

- The woman originates in the man; the man develops through the woman. Neither stands alone.

- Words are spiritual containers. God's Word is powerful and, since we are created in His image, our words are also powerful.

- Men's and women's brains are uniquely designed to fulfill their God-given purposes.

- One of our jobs as a "helper" is prayerfully to assist our mate in learning how to share his heart.

- God's perfect will is brought about when men and women work together, respecting one another's strengths and weaknesses.

Chapter 4

Containers of Power

When God brought Eve to Adam for the first time, Adam was taken aback by her beauty.

"Whoa, man!" he exclaimed breathlessly. The moniker stuck so she is called "wo-man."

Dumb joke. My next two statements may sound equally dumb because they are so obvious: (1) Men are visually attracted to women. (2) Women have power in the image they present to men.

What is not as self-evident is that God created men and women in this way in order to accomplish His purposes in their relationships with each other. To know how to exercise the power God has given us as women, again we need to examine our purpose.

One of God's purposes for men to be attracted to women is to draw men into the matters of the heart. Another purpose is so he will be willing to reproduce. Another is to motivate him visually toward holy living. When a man is attracted to a Christ-centered woman, she has power to lead him into spiritual purity, producing a cleansing effect on his life.

Men in general are more motivated by sight and women are more motivated by hearing, studies tell us. This difference helps each sex achieve its purpose. Man is motivated by sight, which aids his power of authority in the seen world. A woman's motivation by hearing corresponds to her role as a communicator, and aids her power of influence over the unseen world.

Again, it is different yet equal. When women mistakenly believe that the male's role is the more powerful, they may abandon their God-given purposes to vie for the role of authority, and end up stripped of their divinely-ordained power. In frustration they may try to compete even harder, yet remain unfulfilled and even more frustrated. For years our society has applied a double-standard in regard to women, but we females create a new double-standard when we try to compete with males on their level, yet still expect them to treat us like "ladies."

God has an ordained assignment and an established place of authority for women. As we turn our attention to our God-ordained influence and allow ourselves to be containers of the Word of the Lord, we see our power unleashed, feel its effects in all our divinely appointed assignments and are fulfilled in the results that power brings us.

The power God has given the woman to motivate a man through her image is meant to achieve a divine purpose. As the man watches the woman, she is able to influence him into spiritual growth and to motivate him toward spiritual purity. God's Word is a "cleansing" Word. Jesus, the Living Word, came to forgive our sins, and also to cleanse us from all unrighteousness.[1] Carrying the Word of God within our uniquely structured brains and spirits brings a cleansing effect which influences the world around us. Let me explain this further then give the practical applications.

The Old Testament teaches us God's ways in stories and symbols. The laver in the Old Testament was a large wash basin set on a pedestal that stood in the courtyard in front of the Tabernacle. Priests were required to cleanse themselves in the laver before entering the Holy Place after a sacrifice was made. The intriguing part is that the laver was made with the "looking glasses" of the women who assembled at the door of the tabernacle.[2]

A friend of mine was reading her Bible one day when the verse about the laver "leaped out" at her. She called me long distance.

"Mary Jean," she said, "why did God take women's looking glasses from them when Moses collected such a wealth of offerings that he had to stop the people from giving? Why didn't he use what he had already collected to make the laver?"

Good question and great timing. A few weeks later she drove a good distance to attend a seminar Jack and I held that addressed that very topic.

Those contributing "looking glasses" were not ordinary women, but those who "assembled at the door of the Tabernacle."[3] In other words, these women were serious about God. They were assembled at the doors waiting for the opportunity to serve the Lord, not themselves. Today, we would know them as Christ-centered women who earnestly pay attention to the Word of God and who sincerely desire to fulfill God's plan for their lives in order to bring glory and honor to Him. Their "looking glasses" are a symbol of vision or revelation.[4]

These looking glasses were used at a place where men came to cleanse themselves. Still today God uses the "looking glasses" of His women. The vision we portray about God holds great potential to cleanse others. Realizing this great power we hold, we must stop to ponder occasionally what we have in our spirits and minds that reflects outwardly. We must examine ourselves as to what kind of revelation we have of God's Word, and whether we are reflecting an image that brings glory to us or to God.

As we live out our spirit and thoughts in front of others, we exercise our power of influence. Other people can be won to Jesus just by observing His reflection in our lives.[5] As we spend time in God's Word we become containers of God's words, absorbing them, meditating on them and reflecting them. Speaking those words brings salvation and healing to people. Living those words can also bring salvation and healing.

A woman I know has prayed for several years for her husband to be saved. I have seen her in various Bible studies I have led and at different churches around town. Whenever I encounter this woman I find her rallying others for prayer support to save this lost man. For years I felt sympathy and empathy for her until one day I realized that she was at a different church, mingling with a different crowd, every time we met. The Holy Spirit ministered to my heart that the vision this woman portrayed to her husband was flighty, not steadfast in the love of God. She had a faulty belief that the prayers of others would save her lost mate, instead of embracing the Word that says he can be won without a word by observing the chaste behavior of his wife.[6] She is trying to gain "prayer power" but is abandoning the marvelous avenue of power spelled out in God's Word through her very own reflection of Christ.

Generally it is words, spiritual containers, that unlock a woman's mind, whereas a man's mind is unlocked by images. When a man sees a woman living out God's Word, he is motivated by the sight of her more than by any words she speaks. In the same way, as the Church (in the female role) lives out the life of Christ before the world, the world can be won to the Lord.

The Word of God, whether lived out by action or spoken in words, is powerful.[7]

Remember that we cross back and forth between male and female roles as we live out our daily lives. At any given time we may provide a motivating vision for someone, and others can provide it for us. When Jack assisted our pastor, he was our authority in the home until he left for work. Then I became the authority in the home and Jack became a "helper" to his pastor. During the course of his day, however, he interacted with others for whom he again assumed the male or authority role. This is exactly what Jesus did on earth, crossing back and forth easily from authority to influence, maintaining complete peace in every role He assumed.

Another part of our purpose as the "cleansing element" and holder and reflector of God's Word is that we have dominion over the unseen world. Many fine Christian teachers have helped believers understand that God has given all believers dominion over the unseen world as well as the seen world. I believe that for the woman this is true in a special way.

Going back to that first chapter of Genesis, we see that God created the sun, moon and stars.[8] According to the Bible, the sun has dominion over the day, and the moon has dominion over the night. I believe the creation of these "two lights" symbolically foreshadowed the separation of the sexes. The male has the power of authority, which exercises decision-making mastery over the seen world which he is by nature attracted to. The female has the power of influence, which includes sensitivity to and authority over the unseen world which she is by nature attracted to.

Young Joseph dreamed about the sun, moon and stars bowing down to a single star. When he shared his dream with his father, the patriarch Jacob immediately recognized the significance of the dream. Jacob was the sun, his wife was the moon and the stars were Joseph's brothers.[9] Hundreds of years later the psalmist wrote that the glory of God is revealed in the heavens, comparing the glory of the sun to the glory of a bridegroom.[10] In the New Testament, Paul wrote that the man is the glory of God and the woman is the glory of the man.[11] God has revealed His glory in a similar way in the skies and in the sexes. Although I don't want to draw this point out to a ridiculous conclusion, I believe from creation forward the moon symbolizes the female part while the sun symbolizes the male part.

The moon controls ocean tides, which are the cleansing element for our planet. Because of this action, the moon is sometimes referred to as the "maid" of the universe. (Sound familiar?) The tides provide oxygen for the plankton (the foundation of the food chain) and also mix the chemicals that constitute our atmosphere, which makes the moon necessary for the maintenance of life on earth.[12] The moon also provides light. It has dominion over the night, which symbolizes the unseen world. The sun has dominion over the day, or the seen world.

Men, being more focused, less attuned to inner things and more motivated by what they see, are uniquely qualified to rule the seen world. Women, being full of spiritual words and more moved by what they feel and hear, are uniquely qualified to rule the unseen world.

Women's power over the spirit realm and their ability

to motivate others make women extremely important in relationships and in society as a whole. Someone once said, "The moral state of the nation depends on the spiritual state of the women." I believe this statement is true. Women who are not Christ-centered can be a damper on the moral climate wherever they may be. Christ-centered women bring a blessing no matter where they are.

As Christian women, our spirits speak volumes. There is an adornment far richer and greater than the clothes we wear. It is the adornment of the Holy Spirit.[13] We would do well to worry less about putting on attractive and fashionable clothes, and concern ourselves with putting on a gentle and quiet spirit. Think of Mother Teresa and her ministry in India. Numbers of male journalists, missionaries and politicians have been drawn into good works by observing her quietly and unobtrusively going about her Father's business.

We may think, "Well, I could never do what Mother Teresa does."

In fact, you can, and so can I. As women of God, we motivate people every day on a smaller scale for we hold within us the same power of influence that is found in living "saints" like Mother Teresa.

In marriage, our power is even more absolute. The Lord placed a strong attraction in each sex for the other. When the man and woman are in God's will, the woman reveals her heart to the man. As he listens to her, he begins to understand himself better and draws closer to the part of the image of God he sees manifested in her. As the woman shares her heart and submits to the man's headship, she understands herself better and draws closer to the part of God that is revealed through the male. In this way, they complement and complete one another and become "one" in spirit. The sexual relationship becomes the celebration of this intimacy. As an outer expression of deeper spiritual truths, sex belongs in the framework of the marriage covenant established by God.

As you can see, a woman's power is tremendous in scope and in importance, but we have used it for such poor purposes! We women are able to lift an eyebrow, purse our lips or give a little squeak, and each of those tiny gestures translates into power. At the beach a man will walk barefoot across burning sand without flinching just because of a flirtatious look from a bikini-clad woman. That is power! I would never win a bikini contest, but I must confess that I have misused my female power on occasion.

When we women use our inherent power for selfish purposes, we pervert what God gave us to complete and establish our families. Think of the perversions of our power in the sexual realm. Scores of women have been lured into trading their God-given virtue for short-term feelings of warmth, self-worth and power. Rather than adorning a gentle spirit, they have robed themselves in sexually beguiling clothes seeking to entice and motivate men. In so doing, they have become objects of lust and reflections of men's basest animal instincts.

Just as the sight of a holy woman can motivate a man to be holy, so the sight of a sexually perverse woman can motivate a man to be sexually perverse.

I am not saying that it is the woman's fault that some men are lustful. The Bible says that a man is drawn away by *his own* lusts.[14] That men are motivated visually has simply been an excuse for their sinful behavior. However, we women can keep from adding to a man's lust by minding our outward image.

Some women have become harlots, unwittingly. If a man will accept a woman's heart, and enter into covenant with her, she can give him her body. But if she gives him her body and not her heart, according to the Bible she is a harlot.[15] Many women have been deceived into thinking that they need to give their bodies in order to "catch" a man. In truth, a man desires to be known, to become vulnerable and intimate, just as much as the woman does, but he has difficulty doing so unless the woman draws him out. When the woman draws him to her heart, the fruit of that encounter is the coming together of their bodies.

The well-known "Proverbs 31 woman" is the epitome of feminine purity, while the less-discussed "Proverbs 7 woman" is the epitome of uncleanness. She is a woman who gives her body but not her heart. She entices a man into sexual relationship, then wipes her mouth and says she has done nothing wrong.[16] She may desire love, but is ignorant of spiritual truths, or she may simply desire to control the man with her influence. In either case, the result will be the same in that she will not achieve true, lasting fulfillment.

One night a hardened young woman was interviewed on a television talk show. She talked rather brusquely about men and her experiences with them. A man on the program tried to interject something tender and she snapped at him, "If you're expecting me to do an emotional strip, I won't." What she meant was that she refused to reveal her inner heart to the man. She would not let any light come into or through her to be reflected into the outside realm. She had been hurt, had become bitter and now wanted no part in discovering or fulfilling her unique feminine role and purpose.

This same woman might strip her outer body and give it to a man, but she stoutly resisted stripping or revealing her inner heart. In such a case, there is really no communication between the man and the woman, because there is no place for the complementary spiritual parts to connect as God intended.

When a woman does not require a man to hear her heart, she actually defrauds him of his purpose. If she manipulates and gains control over him, she emasculates him. Our society today is full of aggressive women and their male counterparts — weak, dominated men. Such males are far out of God's plan. The Bible says that the man will leave his father and mother and "cleave" (*cling*) to his wife,[17] meaning to attach himself strongly to her.

"When the man cleaves to the woman, it means he is never to stop chasing her," is how one preacher paraphrased this passage.

Today, however, women's aggressiveness is crippling men. As a mother whose phone rang day and night for twelve long years while my sons grew through their teens, I know how aggressive women are today. God has created the man to respond to what he sees, and he is supposed to respond to the woman by pursuing her. As she allows him to "catch" her and submits to his headship, she enables him to develop decisively as a male. But when it is woman who is doing the chasing, she is the one in control. As a result of rapidly changing values and behaviors, our society has been robbed of the foundational development in the different roles of the sexes today, which has led to the confused "androgynous," "unisex" and "homosexual" lifestyles.

Men have their own set of pitfalls. When things go wrong in a relationship, as long as the sexual relationship is still functioning, the man may assume that everything is fine. The sexual relationship is generally the man's barometer of the relationship, whereas the woman's barometer is the level of communication.

A man with lust in his heart can suddenly become a pretty fast talker. Just as the woman attracts the man by her image and appearance, so she is attracted to him by his words, his provision, his care for and cherishing of her. As a result, she naturally reveals her heart to him. This is why some women are deceived by men who have a way with words. Regardless of the negative facts the woman senses or hears about the man and his lifestyle, she may still respond to the seductive words he uses when they are all alone.

Men can become consumed with lust, not love. The husband who does not control his sexuality will not love his wife properly. This lack of control in turn will retard his development emotionally and spiritually. If his wife continually responds to his sexual lust, she will find herself caught up in a cycle of carnality with an immature male. A husband's desire for his wife as an object of sexual lust is not criminal, but is offensive in the eyes of God.[18]

Jesus sets us free from this mess!

If a woman is married to a lustful man, she may become frightened at her own vulnerability as she shares her heart. He may laugh at her, get angry at her, think she is stupid or just refuse to pay any attention to her. For a woman, being ignored perhaps hurts most of all. This is why women are told in Scripture not to fear.[19] As we do our part in faithful obedience to God, He will do His part and bring internal changes.

The Spirit of Christ will help us recognize lust in our husbands and enable us not to feed it, but to bring our husbands out of it. As a husband is drawn to his wife, she can help him submit his sexual drive to her emotional needs. Sometimes a man's carnal desires start when he is very young. Early sexual activity stimulates his flesh and sets him into a lustful cycle. When he marries, he may continue in this selfish, destructive pattern unless his wife becomes his "helper" in learning to love, not lust. Being a helper requires a strong commitment, but it has enduring rewards.

If you are caught up in a cycle of lust, you may match your husband externally, yet miss the intimacy of the marriage covenant internally. If he is not at the place where he is willing to listen to your heart, the situation can still change. You can minister to him with your body and slowly begin to draw him into the hidden things of the spirit. If we minister with our bodies, but require nothing with our hearts, we rob our husbands of their own development. If we minister with our bodies and slowly begin to reveal our hearts, our husbands will respond to the sexual relationship and begin to open, even if only slightly at first, spiritually and emotionally.

To be intimate really means to share on a deeply personal level. Although our society describes sexual relations as intimate, we clearly see that sex exists apart from true intimacy. Any sexual relationship that is not based on an inner sharing of hearts can never truly be intimate.

A harlot gives her body and hides her heart. A godly woman gives her body, then unveils her heart to draw out the male and help him develop and mature. By her actions and appearance, she is getting into position to help her husband in matters of the heart. Instead of complaining to him or God, she is wielding the power God has given her to achieve part of her purpose.

A woman left one of our seminars one day and purposed in her heart to "minister" with her body to her unsaved husband when she got home. She called me later asking when our next meeting was scheduled because her husband actually encouraged her to attend more often!

- Women have power in the image they present to men.

- When a woman becomes the competition, not the completion of the man in a relationship, there is bound to be trouble.

- As we women turn our attention to our God-given influence and allow ourselves to be containers of the Word of God, we will see our power unleashed.

- As we live out our spirit and thoughts in front of others, we exercise our power of influence.

- The Word of God, whether lived out by action or spoken in words, is powerful.

- Words, spiritual containers, unlock a woman's mind, whereas images unlock a man's.

- Just as the sight of a holy woman can motivate a man to be holy, so the sight of a sexually perverse woman can motivate a man to be sexually perverse.

- As women of God, we can and do motivate people every day on a smaller scale than Mother Teresa for we hold within us the same power of influence that is in her.

- A man desires to be known, to become vulnerable and intimate, just as much as the woman does, but he has difficulty doing so unless the woman draws him out.

- As the woman reveals her heart to the man, he listens to her and begins to understand himself better, and draws closer to the part of the image of God he sees manifested in her. As the woman shares her heart and submits to the man's headship, she understands herself better and draws closer to the part of God that is revealed through the male.

- The sexual relationship is generally the man's barometer of a relationship, whereas the woman's barometer is the level of communication.

- It is the sharing of hearts, not bodies, that produces true intimacy.

Chapter 5

The Wise Woman

Every animal my family has ever owned has been a male — Duke, Scooter, Tutu (for whom we paid too, too much). And they all seemed to act like human males. With Jack and the three boys, and their tendency to surround themselves with more males, I have had lots of opportunity to learn the male perspective. Through the years of searching out my place as the odd "man" out, I am happy that at least a little wisdom has entered my heart and mind. God has been good in teaching me to exercise this wisdom, not just expound it, as I deal with my family and others.

One day Charlie was very upset about something. I immediately started to spout off some great pearl of wisdom that would solve his dilemma. But he saw me open my mouth and stopped me before I uttered a word.

"I don't want to know what is the wise thing to do right now!" he snapped.

He just wanted to be mad for awhile. Although I ached to see him go through his painful ordeal, I could remember times when I had told the Lord the same thing Charlie told me. I just wanted to be mad before I got back on my knees. How wise God is in dealing with us. How wise we must be in dealing with others, both to understand correctly and to act at the right moment. Timing can be the difference between wisdom and folly.

As one who holds God's words, the woman is designed to be a vessel of God's wisdom. The woman who sets her heart on Jesus Christ will begin to embody wisdom. There are remarkable similarities in the Scriptures between wisdom and woman.

The Bible says that the value of a virtuous woman is far above that of rubies,[1] which means that Christ-centered women are literally priceless. The Bible gives the same value to wisdom, saying that it is more precious than rubies.[2] Solomon said in his proverbs that happy is the man who "finds" wisdom and "gains" understanding[3] and that whoever "finds" wisdom "finds" life.[4] Later he said that whoever "finds" a wife "finds" a good thing.[5] He continues using the same words, in what I believe is an alliteration, in referring to a connection between women and wisdom. Later the Apostle Peter mirrored this same thought in admonishing husbands to "dwell" with their wives "according to knowledge."[6]

Some teachers have made a hard and fast connection here, but a more basic truth is that women, along with all believers, are exhorted to gain wisdom. If we women truly lived out our primary purpose of building a relationship with God through embracing His Word, which is the source of all wisdom, our husbands (or pastors and others in the male role) could read the following passage and insert our name every time the word "wisdom" is mentioned:

> "Get wisdom, get understanding: forget it not; neither decline from the words of my mouth. Forsake her not, and she shall preserve thee: love her, and she shall keep thee. Wisdom is the principal thing; therefore get wisdom: and with all thy getting get understanding. Exalt her, and she

shall promote thee: she shall bring thee to honour, when thou dost embrace her. She shall give to thine head an ornament of grace: a crown of glory shall she deliver to thee."[7]

With our potential to be such a blessing, we need to gain wisdom, then become someone others *want* to embrace and cherish! By loving others first, we enable them to love and cherish us in return. Love is one of our greatest avenues of power because love never fails. When I am loving to my husband, giving of myself to benefit him and desiring from my heart to see him succeed in God's plan for his life, he can hardly bear to have me away from his side. He wants to cherish me and fulfill his God-given role toward me.

The Bible provides Christian wives a checklist for this kind of loving devotion to their husbands:

"Let the wife see that she
respects and
reverences her husband [that she
notices him,
regards him,
honors him,
prefers him,
venerates and
esteems him, and that she
defers to him,
praises him, and
loves and
admires him exceedingly]."[8]

What a way to love! It's like a "to do" list we can look over each day (I keep this list taped to my desk). Loving a husband the way the Bible instructs us to love helps him respond in the way God wants him to respond. This is wisdom in action and is part of the woman's role.

A woman of wisdom will fear the Lord, because the Bible says that the fear of the Lord is the beginning of knowledge,[9] which is the foundation for wisdom. The fear of the Lord is not a literal fear, like being afraid of some dangerous person or animal, but is a deep awe and reverence for Who God really is, the Almighty One. The woman who fears the Lord desires to reject anything evil that would displease Him because of respect for Who He is.

Wise women are women of substance, mature, Christ-centered. They are not the competitor, but the complement and completion of their husbands. They walk alongside him, and let him know they are not against him. The same can be said of singles in their relationship with the authorities God has placed in their lives.

By taking her place alongside the man, the wise woman does not threaten him, but assures him that she is trustworthy. When the man is assured that he can trust the woman, his heart is confident in her.[10]

Even after years of trial and learning, I speak of the wise woman in the third person because I am still attempting to hit that mark in my own life. So many times I wish I had kept quiet instead of opening my mouth with some "word" of wisdom. Such words are "for an appointed season," and I have missed my season many a time. Edwin Louis Cole, the men's minister, says, "Nagging is simply saying the right thing at the wrong time." How true!

I have had to learn not to talk so much that I confuse or overwhelm Jack. And I have had to learn when to talk. Jack loves to watch the evening news on TV, so that is not the time to tell him about my day. Even worse is trying to talk when he is involved in sports. We have both learned to accommodate the other. When he comes home from work, I wait until after the "cool down" period to ask him about his day. Then he ministers to me by doing his best to dredge up the details. But he is in no mood to minister to me when he is still trying to unwind. I have had to learn to trust him and the Lord in him that he will eventually come around and share his experiences and thoughts with me.

During a time when I was teaching an interdenominational Bible study at a hotel, I learned this lesson of patient trust in a dramatic way. One day as I sat studying alone at my kitchen table, I entered a deep time of prayer and saw a mental image of me teaching this Bible study in the sanctuary of a church whose pastor was a friend of ours. I believed that this fantastic revelation was straight from the Lord, so I was very excited about it.

"Jack, guess what!" I told him that night. "I have a strong impression that I'm going to teach the Bible study at Ric's church!"

Was I ever crushed when Jack responded that it was a terrible idea and he was certain Ric wouldn't even consider renting his sanctuary to us. Quite a struggle ensued internally because I felt I was getting a distinct message from God, but my "authority" wouldn't agree to it. As I turned to the Lord in prayer, I decided that my first priority was to obey God's call to be Jack's "helper," so I set the idea aside.

Weeks later I was again in prayer and again the image of teaching in that sanctuary came to me as fresh and real as the first time. I mentioned it to Jack, but again he was negative. This reaction heightened my internal struggle, but I was determined to win. I remembered how Eve in the Garden of Eden became a "self-worker," not consulting with her covenant partner before partaking of the fruit, and I purposed in my heart to set myself in agreement with my husband. I figured that if God was powerful enough to give Mary Jean Pidgeon a vision, He was well able to bring that vision to reality if He chose to do so! Instead of presuming that I could help God make His dreams come true, I decided simply to be the helper to my husband that the Lord had asked me to be long before I ever saw any vision.

Six months after I had originally approached Jack on this subject, I still felt impressed of the Lord that we were to move the location of our Bible class. Jack and I were in the car going out to dinner one night when I felt I would burst if I didn't mention the topic again.

"Jack, I'm only bringing this up because it keeps coming to me, and I accept your input," I said. "I still see us moving the Bible study over to Ric's church and holding it in the sanctuary there."

"That's a great idea!" Jack said as if he'd never heard it before.

I almost fell out of the car!

This experience taught me a great lesson about timing. When the timing is right, God will bring the man and woman, or authority and influence, into agreement. The result of our agreement was that we approached our friend Ric, he consented, and the Bible study flourished at his church for two years.

Agreement is an important avenue of a woman's power. The Bible says that if any two "agree" on something, it shall be done.[11] Agreement releases power for achievement.

I don't know what would have happened if I had followed my dream without Jack. I don't know whether the pastor would have agreed, whether the Bible study would have been blessed, whether my act of rejecting Jack's advice would have hurt my relationship with him, or anything else. But I do know that the results from waiting on God were pleasing to the Lord, to me, to Jack, to the pastor and to everyone in the Bible study. It is worth the wait to be in agreement with our leadership or mate. God's guidelines are all intended for us to succeed, not fail, in our marriage, our work, our ministry or in any other relationship or endeavor. As women of God, we are led toward success through the wisdom He gives us.

The Bible says that a "prudent" wife is from the Lord.[12] A "prudent" wife, or woman, is one who is wise, understanding and "circumspect," meaning that she is attentive to everything.[13] She watches in all directions to guard against error or danger, especially in the unseen world. When a man has the influence of a prudent wife, the Lord gives him favor.[14] If we want a man with favor, we would be wise to see that we do our part by being a woman of wisdom.

God possessed wisdom before anything else. Before there was earth, or any other created thing, there was wisdom.[15] Wisdom precedes, and prepares us for, that which is to come. The one who searches for and embraces wisdom may know things before they happen. Often it is the woman who holds this place of "seer," exercising her "woman's intuition" as she circumspectly absorbs the things in the spirit realm. This is part of her purpose and an important avenue of her power.

When we women walk in wisdom, wisdom will often stir deep within us. When I "saw" myself teaching in a new setting, before it was time for such a change to come to pass, that vision set me in the direction that I needed to walk in. The rest I had to work out in partnership with my husband. The wise woman witnesses something in her spirit, walks in that direction and waits for the Lord to bring others into agreement.

Going back to our primary purpose of worshiping God, we worship Him by acknowledging Him, serving Him and rejoicing in Him. When we are rejoicing in what the Lord is doing, we don't strive to make His plans come into being. We simply rejoice knowing that wisdom will do its own work in its own way and in its own time.

"The tongue of the wise useth knowledge aright: but the mouth of fools poureth out foolishness."[16]

"The lips of the wise disperse knowledge: but the heart of the foolish doeth not so."[17]

- Timing can be the difference between wisdom and folly.

- Love is one of our greatest avenues of power because love never fails.

- Loving our husband the way the Bible instructs us to love him will help him respond in the way God wants him to respond.

- The woman who fears the Lord desires to reject anything evil that would displease Him because of respect for Who He is in His holy majesty.

- By taking her place alongside the man, the wise woman does not threaten him, but assures him that she is trustworthy.

- When the timing is right, God will bring the man and woman, or authority and influence, into agreement.

- As women of God, we are led toward success through the wisdom He gives us.

- Wisdom precedes, and prepares us for, that which is to come.

- The wise woman witnesses something in her spirit, walks in that direction and waits for the Lord to bring others into agreement.

Chapter 6

Find a Place and Fill It

When my sons visit a video arcade, they gravitate to the action games with sports, wars, cars, martial arts or something high-tech that in some way resembles their lives, or their dreams of life. The game that more closely resembles my life is the low-tech hit-the-gopher game. The player has a large rubber mallet and faces a game table that is covered with holes. Whenever a little plastic creature pops his head out of a hole, the player tries to bean him with the mallet before he pops back down. As the gophers pop up faster and faster, the player has to react quicker and quicker.

Hammering things back into place, trying to anticipate where the next problem will pop up, and getting to it in the nick of time, is a lot like juggling members of a family, a career and even volunteer jobs at a church. Anytime you work with people you soon learn that once one problem is solved another seems to surface.

God has given us a huge mallet to use to handle the ugly things that crop up in life, but it's not a physical weapon. Interceding in prayer is the spiritual way to hammer things back into place. The prerequisite for exercising the power of intercession, however, is to stand in position. No matter how wildly you swing that rubber mallet, you won't hit anything if you have walked away from the game table.

For years the positions of male and female have competed with each other, bringing about ugly conflicts and problems. In God's Kingdom there is no jockeying for position, since everything He creates fills a unique niche. God doesn't create two things to occupy the same place. He is not the author of confusion,[1] but of order. If God created woman for a specific purpose, then the most powerful place she can be is in position to accomplish that purpose.

When we are properly positioned and set on fulfilling our purpose, we have power. Jesus told His disciples that He had chosen them and placed them in position to go out and "bear fruit." Immediately after making this statement, He said that whatever they asked of His Father, in His name, God would give it to them.[2]

When the enemy of God's Kingdom, Satan, wishes to short circuit the power of the Lord in our lives, the first method he seems to employ is to get us out of position. He does this through deceit, pressure and distractions. Once out of position, we are almost powerless against him. A soldier out of position in a physical battle leaves himself open to attack, as well as weakening the entire line. Likewise, our poor position and lack of power weaken the part of the Body of Christ, or Army of God, to which we are joined. It is vital to find our position and stay in it if we wish to see victory in our lives, our families, our churches and our sphere of influence. The unique position of the female gives her the power to bring her to the ultimate end of overcoming the evil one, which translates into glory to God.

Women are constantly being exposed to a rebellious attitude, and enticed by those who want them to join in that rebellion. Ever since the Garden of Eden, when God pronounced to Satan, "I will put enmity between you and the woman, and between your seed and her seed,"[3] there has existed a prejudice against women. We females have been targeted by the devil who has attacked us through the attitudes and actions of his followers, usually hitting us right where we are weakest, right where we hurt most. Like Eve, we are highly susceptible to his attacks. But, God says that the "seed" of the woman will win! The issue is already resolved. Jesus Christ came into this world through a woman, and it is through His death and resurrection that the power of sin and Satan is forever broken off those of us who believe in Christ as our Savior. We just need to get into position and lay hold of the resurrection power of God that turns presumptions, pressures and prejudice into our greatest life victories.

The tendency of the world is to flow comfortably and easily down Satan's maniacally driven stream that eventually leads into his sea of grief, despair and turmoil. When we arrest that flow to fill our God-given position, we may find it difficult at first. But once we are securely in place, we discover that God's power flows through us and Jesus is all around us, loving, protecting and leading us all the way.

Old Testament physical battles foreshadow New Testament spiritual battles. One of my favorite verses, and one of the most encouraging in the Bible dealing with obstacles, is the one in which the Lord told His people, "You will not need to fight in this battle. Position yourselves, stand still and see the salvation of the Lord, who is with you."[4]

Position yourselves! If we find our position, the battle is half won already. When we stand in our position, God gets involved in our lives and brings forth victories.

Position is crucial to winning a battle.

Through the years, I have learned that cutting off the

old flow of life and getting situated in proper spiritual position involves a constant daily attitude adjustment. We already looked at the man in marriage as the "head." For years I struggled with the seeming unfairness of that truth. If Jack is my head, I thought, what does that leave for me to be? I finally learned that when my husband is the head, that leaves me to be the whole rest of the body!

> "But I would have you know, that the head of
> every man is Christ; and the head of the woman is
> the man; and the head of Christ is God."[5]

"Headship" is part of the male role which constantly shifts and interplays with the complementary female role. Although our role as women may shift into "headship" when we enter an area in which we exercise authority, God has placed the male in the role of headship in the home and family. This is not a headship that allows "bullying," but one patterned after the headship of the caring, gentle Christ.

A very intelligent friend complained one day about how hard it was to lose weight. "Oh well," he sighed, "God just made my body to hold up my brain anyway."

In a sense, that is true. Heads need bodies to hold them up! This is where we fit positionally.

Once I accepted the headship of my husband, I was tempted severely to compete against that role and try to occupy it myself. One time specifically I faced a dilemma over something as mundane as Charlie's birthday party. The little neighbor boy, Josh, was one of Charlie's closest playmates, and their circle of friends was identical. Josh's birthday was one day after Charlie's, and every year his mother and I dealt with the conflict of scheduling parties. This particular year, Josh's mother planned his party on

Charlie's birthday. When she told me, I didn't say anything but mentally noted to celebrate Charlie's birthday a day late. When I ran this idea past Jack, he emphatically said, "No. Charlie will celebrate his birthday on his birthday."

Instantly I was in a quandary as to what to do. When Josh's mother had alerted me to his party, I had said nothing so she went ahead with her plans. Planning Charlie's party now according to Jack's instructions would ruin our friendship. And relationships with our neighbors were far more dear to me than they were to Jack, because I was the one who had to deal with them. After I cooled down toward Jack a little, I went into my room to pray. While talking to the Lord, I felt distinctly that to go against my husband's wishes would be to lose my position beside him. After years of fighting to discover, then fill, the "helper" position, I was just bull-headed enough not to want to lose it!

After tears, groans and finally a sense of completion, I left my place of prayer feeling assured in my heart that I needed to fill my position with my husband, even at the expense of good relations with my neighbors. I knew somehow that God would make it up to me, although I was completely unaware of the power we unleash when we hold fast to the place the Lord has given us. The next morning at eight o'clock, Josh's big sister rang my doorbell. When I opened it, there she stood, holding a note from her mother. In the note my neighbor said that she had awakened at 3:00 A.M. and realized that she had planned Josh's party on Charlie's birthday. Embarrassed, she was writing to inform me that she would be changing all her plans to have Josh's party the day following Charlie's.

This was a small issue, but a great lesson revealing to me the tremendous power the Lord would use on my behalf if I would just hold fast to my position. God was infinitely more capable of changing that woman's mind than I ever gave Him credit for. I realized that if the Lord is that faithful to me even in trivial circumstances, what good things must He have planned for me when it comes to the truly important issues?

The power of God is released when we are in position, whether we are occupying the position of authority or influence. The key is finding the position God has for us at a specific time and filling it. According to the Scriptures, *no good thing will He withhold from those who walk uprightly.*[6] That's a promise that makes getting into position worth the effort.

When leadership is weak or wicked, or when we question the leader's decisions, we end up in a dilemma. Whether leaders are weak or wicked or wrong, it is all the same. Each variance from God's will gives Satan a foothold in that leader's life and therefore affects his or her decisions. I have learned both through experience and Scripture that intercession is the answer. When we intercede, God's Spirit is released to work supernaturally in the situations we bring to Him.

Abigail's life in the Old Testament illustrates this principle. Abigail is a real historical woman who met King David before he was crowned king. She was a virtuous woman, of "good understanding" and "beautiful countenance."[7] Unfortunately, her husband, Nabal, was a wicked fool. The Bible is very blunt about this fact.

One day David sent some of his men to Nabal to ask for provisions. David's men had protected Nabal's servants and possessions while his sheep grazed, and now that it was sheep-shearing time, David expected something in return, which was customary in those days. But Nabal treated David's men disrespectfully and sent them away empty-handed. When David heard of this insult, he rose in a rage, put on his sword and ordered his men to prepare for battle to destroy Nabal's house and all who were found in it.

In Bible typology, David represents the anointed of God. By being disrespectful to David, Nabal was really being disrespectful to God.

Nabal's servants went to Abigail and told her, "Evil is determined against our master, and against all his household."[8] Because of his wrong attitude and actions, Nabal had unleashed evil against himself and his entire house.

When she was informed of the situation, Abigail quickly took offerings with her and sent servants ahead to intercept the invaders without her husband's knowledge. Coming to David herself, Abigail fell on her face and cried, "Upon me let this iniquity be: and let thine handmaid, I pray thee, speak."[9] She went on to admit that her husband Nabal was a wicked man and a fool, begging forgiveness for the offense. She reasoned with David that if he would relent of his anger and repent of his planned vengeance, then someday when he was king, he would not have this past tragedy to regret. She pointed out that perhaps God was protecting David from the deed by sending her to intervene. David immediately agreed.

Seeing a leader in the wrong is no great shock. We can see the weaknesses of our husbands, the mistakes of our pastors, the errors of corporate officers and even the dishonesty of our government leaders. But Abigail did something about what she saw. Instead of going up against the wrong or wicked leader, Abigail took the sin upon herself and positioned herself in front of her family in intercession to protect them from the offended party. First Abigail forgave, then she asked God for forgiveness. When she took it upon herself to ask for forgiveness, she turned away the danger that threatened her household. Forgiveness is a tremendous avenue of power for us.

I can think of many other things Abigail could have done instead of interceding with David. She must have been disgusted with Nabal, and could have washed her hands of the whole affair, declaring in bitterness, "It serves him right."

Or, she could have gone to Nabal and told him off, spending her energies trying to convince him that he was wrong and she was right. Of course, while they were arguing, David might have arrived and killed everyone.

What Abigail didn't do was get involved in laying blame or arguing about the situation. She went beyond all the surface issues to the heart of the real problem — and then dealt with it. What a woman!

The story concludes with Nabal dropping dead of an apparent stroke or heart attack and David taking the newly widowed Abigail as his wife.

God deals with leaders in His own time when we get out of His way and pray.

Today we have the opportunity of knowing Jesus Who died for the sins of the whole world. Through His death and resurrection He has positioned us to receive even greater power than Abigail enjoyed. Jesus bore our pain and carried our sorrow in His body. Every sin, sickness and iniquity was atoned for at the Cross. Whatever sin we have to deal with, whether in ourselves or in someone else, Jesus has already covered in His sacrificial death at Calvary. He has atoned for every sin we have committed, every sin committed against us and every sin others have committed. To get right with Him, all we have to do is to apply that forgiveness through repentance and prayer.

The offerings Abigail took David represent the blood Jesus freely offered from His own body to cover our sins. When we encounter weakness, wickedness or wrongdoing, we can take what Jesus did for us and ask God to forgive the sins of all involved in the situation, covering them with the blood of Jesus. Our offering is no longer something we gather up from ourselves, but it is the offering Jesus freely provided for us, which more than compensates for every sin.

God does not desire for anyone to perish.[10] He desires for all people to be saved.[11] He is looking for Abigails today who will carry His provision for salvation and make intercession for those who are in rebellion against Him. Abigail stepped into a Christlike role when she took upon herself the sins committed by someone else. We do the same when we continue Christ's atoning work here on earth through intercession.

Immaturity is simply the refusal to accept responsibility. Maturity is accepting responsibility for self. But Christlike maturity is accepting responsibility not only for self but for others.[12] Great leaders accept responsibility for the acts of their subordinates. Likewise, although we do not accept the guilt of those around us, we do accept the responsibility to pray in earnest intercession for them.

Abigail forgave Nabal. Then she accepted responsibility for the sins of her husband and submitted them to the Lord by carrying them symbolically to the foot of the Cross. Often women try to continue carrying others' sins, assuming responsibility that is far too great for them to bear. Only

God can handle such a load, which is why He sent His Son to carry the sins of the entire world.

Some try to intercede while still harboring bitterness in their hearts. We must forgive on our behalf, then ask God to forgive. When we turn away from judgment and intercede by asking forgiveness on behalf of the sinner, we can then ask for the light of God to shine into the heart of that person and reveal the truths of His Kingdom to him or her. When we take this position, we see problems solved and people changed.

In sharp contrast to the powerful, Christlike spirit of intercession are actions based on emotions, fleshly desires and revenge. Returning evil for evil, gossiping and tearing down others violates Christ's principles and profits nothing. We must be careful to grow past our own emotions. We must develop to the place that our motivation in prayer is the desire for God's will to be accomplished on earth. For example, perhaps at first we want our husband to be saved just so our lives will be better off, but we must get beyond this selfish attitude to a sincere desire that our husband will be changed so he can better reflect the glory of God. Through this process, we die to our desires[13] and become alive to God's will and purpose. In this position, the power of the Lord is released through us.

One verse in particular sums up God's attitude when we are in the proper position: "And having in a readiness to revenge all disobedience, when your obedience is fulfilled."[14]

God stands ready to punish all disobedience when we have done what is right. People don't necessarily need us to tell them they are weak, wicked or wrong. People desperately need us to intercede for them and turn away God's wrath to give them another chance to surrender themselves or that unsanctified part of their lives to the Lordship of Jesus Christ.

This is a tough lesson, and I know it is not easy to learn. As you take your position and begin to pray, remember these simple words:

Good overcomes evil.[15]

Light dispels darkness.[16]

Life swallows up death.[17]

The Lord will eventually win every victory for you when you are in position. Take your position and see the salvation of the Lord!

- God created woman for a specific purpose, and the most powerful place she can be is in position to accomplish that purpose.

- Jesus Christ came through a woman and through His death and resurrection forever broke the power of sin off those who believe. In position we lay hold of the resurrection power of God that turns problems into victories.

- The power of God is released when we are in position, whether we are occupying the position of authority or influence.

- God deals with leaders in His own time when we get out of His way and pray.

- Position yourselves! If we find our position, the battle is half won already. When we stand in our position, God gets involved in our lives and brings forth victories.

- Christlike maturity is accepting responsibility not only for self but for others.

- Although we do not accept the guilt of those around us, we do accept the responsibility to pray in earnest intercession for them.

- Good overcomes evil.
  Light dispels darkness.
  Life swallows up death.

Chapter 7

Submitting to Power

I was standing in the store laughing out loud while reading a greeting card that I couldn't resist buying for Jack. Though it was hilarious to me, when I brought it home and showed it to Jack, he hardly grunted. Having never been in a woman's position, sometimes men just don't understand. The card read as follows, with the last line on the inside: "First he said he liked independent women, so I played it cool. Then he said he liked romantic women, so I played it hot. Then he said he liked passive women, so I played it weak. Then he said he liked strong women . . . so I crushed his head."[1]

Husbands sometimes don't realize what we women go through in trying to be good wives to them. Part of our inability to communicate and empathize with each other as husbands and wives arises from a misunderstanding of our respective roles. When it comes to being a "head" or "submitting" to one, some men can't muster the courage to become the head and some women can't tolerate the idea of submitting. We've talked about the purpose of headship and the position. Now let's examine the power.

There is a difference between "headship" and "leadership." The Apostle Paul exhorted us to pray "for all men; for kings, and for all that are in authority."[2] The Greek word translated "men" here is *anthropos*, which actually means "*man-faced*,"[3] thus referring to mankind, or human beings, both men and women. Paul understood that women can rightfully step into the role and power of authority. Miriam was a leader along with her brothers Moses and Aaron.[4] Deborah was a judge.[5] Huldah was a counselor.[6] Phoebe was a deaconess.[7]

In the Church, however, only Christ is the head. And in the home, only the man fills the male role as head.[8] A woman can hold a leadership position, but she is never the "head" of a marriage and family. When a man enters a covenant with a woman in marriage he assumes the responsibility of headship and uses his special gifts in that office. A man's unique purpose of headship, like a woman's unique purpose of influence, is carried from the home into the rest of life. In the work place, the man's propensity for headship continues even apart from his family. Instead of competing against this system, a woman can draw from a man's gifts, complete him and thus release both the man and herself into even greater power.

A woman does not need to compete with a man for power. She has her power, he has his, and there is room for both even in large quantities!

The two words from Greek that are translated as "head" in English are *arche* and *kephale*. *Arche* means "boss, magistrate, chief or ruler." *Kephale* refers to the literal head of a body, and means "foremost" in terms of position. *Kephale* also means "one who leads" in a military sense like the first one into battle, not the general who directs the battle from a distance.[9] *Kephale* is the word Paul used in this context.[10] The husband is to be the "first into battle," but is not described as the "boss," much less the bully. The husband is the cornerstone for the family and the one who leads into conflict. He is the outer part, the covering, that is toughened for the job. We have seen that the male brain is specialized to be less distracted, which is a great quality for a "point man."

On the other hand, the woman is to be submissive to this "head," just as her body must submit to her head in order to be effective and to keep from becoming disjointed.

"For after this manner in the old time the holy women also, who trusted in God, adorned themselves, being in subjection unto their own husbands."[11] The holy women of the Bible put on a submissive attitude. The word "submissive" sounds archaic to our modern ears and seems unnatural to our Western minds because it has been greatly misrepresented over the years. There are women who fight against "submitting" to husbands, and others who fight to keep the word "obey" in the marriage vows. Both are partially right, and partially wrong.

The words "be subject to" are used in three different relationships in the famous passage from the Apostle Paul's letter to the Ephesians.

"*Be subject to* one another out of reverence for Christ. Wives, *be subject to* your husbands, as to the Lord. . . . As the church *is subject to* Christ, so let wives also *be subject in everything to* their husbands."[12]

Church members are to be subject to one another. Wives are to be subject to their husbands. The Church is to be subject to Christ. In a group, everyone cannot obey everyone else, so we can be sure that being subject to someone does not necessarily mean to obey that person or this verse would make no sense. Paul's original Greek word that is translated "be subject to" was a term that meant to subordinate oneself *voluntarily*. It did not carry the connotation to obey which Paul used when talking about children with their parents, nor did it mean to dutifully obey as was the case with the word he used for slaves.

One Greek language authority comments, "Since it is asking for something that is voluntary in nature, 'be subject to' is an awkward translation at best. [It really] means something like 'give allegiance to,' 'tend to the needs of,' 'be supportive of,' or 'be responsive to.'"[13]

Another definition would be "to place oneself at the disposition of." This carries a connotation of equality, "an equal sharing of the task" in which one worker allows another to lead in order to accomplish their goals.[14] If you envision a perfect "helper" for someone, you could see the person doing all of the above.

None of these definitions has anything to do with a person's ability. Just because a bookkeeper allows an accountant to oversee her work does not necessarily mean that she is incompetent, but rather that it is expedient for her to avail herself of someone else's time, perspective and expertise to see that everything is done in order.

Neither has any of these definitions anything to do with a person's worth. It does not lower our value to submit to the president of the United States or to an employer or a police officer. Nor is value an issue when a wife submits to a husband or a choir member to the choir leader. When a person feels oppressed by the call to submit, something is out of order. The leader may be bullying, or the person could be feeling devalued in the submissive position.

Some Vietnam veterans gathered several years ago at the home of U.S. Representative John Warner for a breakfast meeting to raise support for the Vietnam Veteran's Memorial in Washington, DC. After they had eaten breakfast and concluded their business, Congressman Warner introduced their chef. Out from the back room walked the woman who had cooked the meal. She was clad in a robe and slippers. It was Warner's wife at the time, Elizabeth Taylor. The military men were reduced to awkward, ogling schoolboys in the presence of this violet-eyed mega-star.[15] Did this woman lose value when she supported the efforts of men by cooking for them? No! She was still Elizabeth Taylor. It's time we start realizing that we are still the same worthwhile person regardless of where we are, whom we support or how we support them.

The power of authority is released when the one in the position of authority makes godly decisions. The power of influence, however, is released when the one in the position of influence displays a willingness to submit to those decisions. Of the two, I believe the most powerful place is found in the position of submission.

When we declared ourselves Christians, we actually declared ourselves to be called "out from among them."[16] We are called out from doing things in the way the world does them. The third chapter of First Peter describes the submissive spirit as part of our Christian walk. The Holy Spirit has a submissive spirit and submits Himself to you and me every day of our lives. He does not rule over us, but helps us; so every day He stands waiting for us to receive His help, submitting to our lack of understanding or our laziness. In other words, He doesn't barge into our lives without our asking. In that way, He submits to our will, however foolishly we may exercise it.

Jesus has a submissive spirit. Jesus' power was released through His submission to the will of the Father that He die for our sins. In the natural realm, Jesus' death appeared to be His weakest moment, as He hung limp and seemingly helpless on a Roman cross. But in His submission to the Cross, Jesus broke the power of the devil over us for all eternity. He submitted to death in the physical realm to pave the way for us to become alive with Him in the spiritual realm.[17] As Christians who are to become more like Jesus we — both male and female — find ourselves most often in the position of submission. When we are in submission to God, the spirit realm opens to us.

Whether male or female, when we submit to God we align ourselves with Christ and release God's power into our lives.[18]

The Apostle Paul desired more of the power of submission rather than the power of authority. He talked freely of what Jesus had taught him. "And he said unto me, My grace is sufficient for thee: for my strength is made perfect in weakness. Most gladly therefore will I rather glory in my infirmities, that the power of Christ may rest upon me."[19]

The word Paul used here for "power" is actually *dunamis* in the original Greek. It literally means: ability, abundance, miraculous power, a miracle itself.[20] When he quoted the Lord as saying "my strength is made perfect in weakness," the word "perfect" literally means complete, accomplish, or consummate; consecrate, fulfill, finish.[21] The word "weakness" literally means feebleness of mind or body, frailty, weakness, sickness, and disease.[22]

If we take these words and re-translate what the Lord told Paul, we could say, "My miracle-working power, My abundance and ability, is accomplished, fulfilled, and consummated in your weakness, feebleness of mind or body, and sickness." Paul realized that when he was at his weakest was when the power of God was the strongest on his behalf. He began to put confidence in the fact that in his weakness God's glory rested upon him and as he flowed with the power of the Lord he would find victory.

Paul was a man who, according to the natural realm, had everything working for him. He was strong in his own abilities, relationships and heritage. But as he walked with God, he found that when he submitted to the will of God and laid aside his own abilities, he tapped into a far greater source of power that touched the lives of all those around him.

Instead of hanging on to selfish ambitions to exercise the power of authority, Paul wholeheartedly embraced the power of submission. His greatest desire became to "know Him [Jesus] and the power of His resurrection, and the fellowship of His sufferings, being conformed to His death."[23]

In other words, Paul wanted to die to his own authority and abilities, and live solely through the power of Jesus Christ generating through him. This captivated him above all that his fame and position as a minister had to offer.

Are you in a situation that you cannot think your way out of, or physically remove yourself from? Great! You qualify for God's power to work through you. As we put ourselves into the seemingly weak position of submission, we qualify for the greatest release of God's power in and through us.

Jesus taught and lived the fact that if we will let go of our own desires and controls, He will lift us up to a higher and much more exciting and rewarding plane of existence. The majority of us live most of our lives on a far lower level than what God intends. We need to deal with the basic sins of life: the lust of the flesh, the lust of the eyes and the pride of life.[24] As we endeavor to overcome sin and Satan, the good news is that we can depend on the power of God arising in our weakness![25]

Sometimes we just have too much pride to step back and allow God's power to flow to and through us. If there is strife and envy because both husband and wife are vying for the "head" position, there is confusion. When workers or politicians are caught up in strife and envy while competing for the spot of "top dog," all kinds of evil is unleashed. Scripture says that where strife and envy are, there is confusion and *every* evil thing.[26] It seems that between the sexes, we have lived out this verse day by day.

I have a stubborn pride in me that God has had to deal with in order for me to learn submission, and Jack hasn't always been the excellent leader he is today. The Lord had to teach me to die to myself, willingly submit to my husband and expect God in His goodness and fairness to take care of me regardless of what Jack did. When I finally bowed my knee to the Word of the Lord by submitting myself to my husband, I learned that God looked on this gesture as an act of love toward Him. Obedience to God is the evidence of love for Him. And obedience becomes another avenue of power.

The results of such obedience were almost unbelievable. I had no anticipation nor forewarning of the tremendous power God would unleash in the lives of my family members nor of the changes He would effect once I bowed my knee and got into a submissive position.

God responded to my love for Him by pouring out His love upon me. I had placed myself under Jack and as God poured out His love upon me it seemed to pass over Jack in a spiritual sense. Jack wasn't sitting in the "splash zone" getting some of the droplets of God's love, but He was right over me getting "the whole bucket" along with me. As a result, Jack got caught up in my love affair with the Lord. Because love never fails, Jack began to develop in the love God had for him.

As God loved me through Jack, and Jack through me, the love we shared as husband and wife grew and enlarged. Once Jack agreed to occupy the position of headship, he began to develop in that position. The overall effect was that he was radically transformed from a church-going businessman into an eager disciple of Jesus Christ. Jack was responsible for making this good decision, not me, but in God's divine order, when any one person falls into line with Him, His power is released in every part of that person's life. Jack's success sequentially followed my conscientious decision to take and hold a submissive position. The changes that came to our family after my act of submission were exactly what I had been harping about for years while operating powerlessly outside my proper position.

We have been robbed of so many good things because of the "pride of life" that won't allow us to submit ourselves willingly to someone else's authority, or to place others first in our lives. We must address such attitudes of the heart if we are to receive all that God has for us. As human beings, we tend to let spiritual things slip, so we must hear the Word preached, read it ourselves and remind one another of it constantly.

The vast difference between man-preached submission and God-intended submission is that one is a suppressive bondage while the other is a release of the miracle-working power of God.

In the passage we quoted about the holy women who

adorn themselves with a submissive spirit, we are encouraged to "do well" and not be afraid "with any amazement."[27] In Greek the word translated "amazement" means to scare or frighten.[28] About what is the Scripture encouraging us not to be frightened? Part of our purpose as a female is to reveal "the hidden man of the heart"[29] and live out the truth in front of the man in our life in relationship with him. But then we must deal with the man's response to us. This can be the scary part.

Men are not always happy to see us women live out the truth. In fact, their responses might be anger, reproach or mockery. When a man sees an object of lust, his response will generally be lustful. But when a man sees a woman of excellence living out God's Word, his response may vary. If he is not walking in the same truth he sees in her, he may avoid her, run from her or become angry with her. His defense might also be to criticize or ridicule her. When he sees in her the truth of God's Word, his response is actually and ultimately aimed at the Holy Spirit, but the woman happens to be in the middle of it. When the man rejects truth, it isn't her he is rejecting, it is the Lord he sees reflected in her. So God the Father says to His daughters, "Don't be worried or afraid." We are to have relationship with Him and then with the man in our life. If it brings about a confrontation, the Lord is with us. As we continue to submit to the Lord, His power will flow through us. In our weakest moment, His power is perfected in us and made strong on our behalf.

Husbands receive a caution from the Lord at the same time:

> "Wives, submit yourselves unto your own husbands, as it is fit in the Lord. Husbands, love your wives, and be not bitter against them."[30]

God cautions the husband against bitterness because as the wife reflects the Spirit of Truth, the Holy Spirit begins to convict him and he may be tempted to take out his reactions on her. When Eve reflected the serpent's lie, Adam's reaction to that act was his responsibility — and he chose to sin. As a godly woman reflects God's glory, her husband's reaction is his responsibility, whether it is to submit to God as he sees her doing, or to rebel in bitterness.

The woman is called to submit "as is fitting in the Lord."[31] If her submission is manipulative or feigned, then it is not "fitting in the Lord" and she is actually challenging her husband's headship. On the other hand, it may be where the man is leading that is not "fitting." The wife may have to explain to her husband that even though she is submitted to him, she cannot follow him because his actions are not legal, moral or ethical. The place where we stop submitting is not where we decide that the man in our life is an unfit leader. The place where we stop submitting is the place where submission violates our faith because "whatever is not from faith is sin."[32]

The word "bitter," as used in Colossians 3:19, can mean distasteful, distressing and distrustful. A man who responds with bitterness to his wife's submission may go through a season in which he is unsettled and in a state of change. He knows his old ways are wrong and he feels vulnerable. His male ego does not like to admit that his wife is right in her behavior. The wife at this point must exercise wisdom and realize what her husband is experiencing. It profits nothing to declare, "That's what I've been saying all along"; in fact, such words and attitude can do great harm. The wife must adopt a gentle and quiet spirit and be supportive and non-judgmental of her husband. She must remember that he doesn't need a judge but an intercessor.

With her silent, prayerful help, he will make the transition and develop as God desires.

When I first met Jesus, I became an avid Bible reader. I didn't know it until later, but my Bible reading angered Jack. He would walk into the kitchen every morning and get irritated to see me with my Bible open because he knew he should be doing the same thing. Yet he never let on that my Bible study had any effect on him at all.

We may not be aware of all that is happening when we get into position. Other times the Lord may reveal it to us. Regardless of what we can or cannot see, we can be sure that God's power is working, so we must hold to that position!

A budding male Christian can use the help of a virtuous woman in relating to being godly. The submissive Christian spirit may be completely foreign to him. By seeing it in her, he may be able to learn how to adopt it himself. By seeing power released in her life, he can be comforted knowing that as he moves into a submissive position to the Lord, God's power will be released in his life as well.

It may be difficult for a husband to think that he can be used by God, but through his wife's submission she can help him see the image of God in himself. This will build him up and give him confidence to go about the work of the Lord. It is a great spiritual principle that as we highlight the good in others, we will see great qualities emerge from them.

One night Jack and I had a meeting with friends at our house. At the end, we all stood around in a circle and prayed. In the midst of Jack's prayer, he changed from making a request to voicing a statement of encouragement from the Lord for all of us. I realized how the Holy Spirit had inspired Jack's words and assumed that he had sensed the same.

Later as we were cleaning up, I casually mentioned it to him.

"That was a great word the Lord gave you for us," I said.

"What word?"

"You know, while you were praying."

"What do you mean? I was just praying."

"Well, you may have started out praying," I said, "but God took over and used you to minister to the people right where we needed it. It was great."

I was a little annoyed at first to have to explain this until I realized that Jack genuinely did not understand what the Lord had done. God had revealed it to me, and it was my role to tell him. He was excited to learn how God had used him and afterwards became more and more bold as he prayed in public.

Such encouragement causes people to grow in spiritual things. We don't have to be preachers or stand in front of a Sunday School class to teach. God uses us right where we are.

Both positions are challenging — the decision-maker and the helper. When a person masters being a helper, he or she can become a good leader. Many men are poor leaders because they have not learned to be good helpers. When the woman learns her role and reflects the helper image to the man, he can learn what truly helps. That knowledge equips him to act in a helping capacity himself.

Sometimes two people work together who are equally strong and have their own separate visions of what needs to be accomplished. In such cases, the one who is rightfully the "helper" in the situation must step aside and assist in the accomplishment of the vision the Lord has given the other person. As a result, God's power is released and the faith of the one who submits is increased.

Jesus equated submission with faith. When a Roman centurion asked Him to heal his servant, Jesus said He would come and heal the man. The centurion told Jesus not to bother coming to his house, but just to speak the word and the servant would be healed. The centurion explained, "I am a man under authority, having soldiers under me: and I say to this man, Go, and he goeth; and to another, Come, and he cometh; and to my servant, Do this, and he doeth it."[33] His answer amazed Jesus.

The centurion recognized that Jesus was submitted to authority, and therefore had power to heal. He realized that just as a word from him caused men to respond because of the authority over him, so a word from Jesus would effect healing in his household because of the authority of God the Father over Him. Jesus was so impressed at this man's understanding of submission that he called it "great faith."[34]

Submitting to God through another person shows a greater measure of faith than submitting to God directly. God is always kind and gentle. He never puts us down, but always encourages us and loves us. He isn't caught up in Himself and full of selfish ambition, so He is easy to love in return. But when we have to deal with someone whose mind is on himself or herself or who puts us down or disagrees with us, that can be tough. When such a person is in authority over us, it takes great faith to submit to that individual, but it also causes us to grow in our faith in the Lord.

I remember a difficult situation with Jack that started out as a blessing and ended up making me stretch and my faith grow.

I was teaching two Bible studies and was active in the singles department of the large church we attended. Jack was an active layman, but was still in the insurance business with no aspiration for full-time ministry. After a great deal of prayer, the singles pastor asked Jack to become the lay coordinator for singles. It was great timing, and events worked out perfectly for Jack to step into that role. I was thrilled because one of my prayers was to work side by side with my husband in ministry. The day Jack accepted the job was a great day for me personally.

Then came the conflicts. Up to that point, I was the sole teacher of the singles, and was an established teacher in the church. This situation gave me free access to the pastoral staff, and my suggestions were always well received. Now suddenly I had to move over and allow Jack to make decisions through his new role of authority that I had formerly held. It was quite a transition for me.

This was when I first began to learn the art of "quietness." My faith was stretched as I stood by and interceded, counseled without pushing and accepted Jack's decisions without judging. Opportunities abounded for me to open my mouth, insist on my way and hurt Jack's feelings — and sometimes I did. After all, I had been there longer than he had. I had to learn how to speak a wise word "in due season,"[35] and withhold comments when they could have been construed as pushy or nagging. Because I exercised self-restraint and allowed the Lord to teach Jack, He was able to do a far better job equipping him for service than I could have done.

Eventually, Jack and I began to team teach. It was amazing to watch God move in such an open and visible way. As I would complete my portion of the lesson and give the microphone to Jack, I would discover that we complemented each other perfectly. The teaching was far more full, potent and applicable when we moved into that role together as a team. The single men responded to Jack in ways they had never responded to me, and likewise the women showed a far greater understanding of the things of God as they experienced our teaching together.

Almost two years later the Lord nudged Jack about selling the business he had spent eighteen years building. Jack submitted to the Lord's call and after seven months became the full-time singles pastor at our church when the former singles pastor stepped down. The exciting life of following Christ was becoming more and more thrilling for us.

During this time a single woman named Annette came to me for counsel. She was an engineer who served as a project manager with several male engineers under her, but she could not rally them to accept her leadership. When she tried stepping back, they ran over her. When she tried applying more force, they complained that she was "bossy."

Being in the throes of learning my own role and position with Jack, I empathized with her and began to teach her the differences in the roles she was playing as a leader of men. She had to learn not to threaten their manhood and yet assume the role of authority in order to get the job done right. As we finished what was to be our last appointment, I simply said, "If you will respect their manhood, Annette, these men will respect you as their boss."

With that advice our meeting ended. A few weeks later before a singles meeting Annette flew through the doors early, bouncing and beaming, to tell me and Jack her joyous news. She had made a conscientious effort to acknowledge each team member's manhood and encourage each of them in their individual strengths during the regular course of a week's work. When it came time for the weekly scheduled meeting that usually brought her so much grief, something fundamental had changed. After tossing around various ideas, she made a decision and the men unanimously agreed. She left the conference room that day almost in shock, but full of joy that she had discovered one of God's principles of life. Annette learned the power of holding her position while retaining respect for others.

Jack and I have now moved in and out of these roles often and each time we readjust ourselves. Jack was used to making his own decisions in business, but then he became one of seven pastors who submitted to a senior pastor. After that experience, he took over the ministry in which I had been occupying the lead role, and finally became a senior pastor by pioneering the church we now serve, West Houston Christian Center. In each role, there was an adjustment to be made. He had to learn just as I did that there are times to be in charge, and times to submit.

Both positions have equal importance. Even more significant, the position itself is not nearly as important as what the person does with it.

Jack and I were able to go to California for a ministry meeting once. This was my first time to see the West Coast, a place I had always wanted to visit. My heart was in my throat during most of the flight. We arrived and went to the baggage claim area where we waited for friends. As I looked out the plate-glass windows, I saw a few palm trees in the distance, but the rest of the terminal just looked like any other so I thought, "Well, an airport is an airport." Our friends came and we crammed into their car and headed down the freeway. Our bags were piled high, and I had a travel bag in my lap that I peered over to see what great things lay just outside my window. I saw cars bustling by, heavy traffic and freeway offshoots spreading in every direction, just like Houston. So I thought, "Well, a freeway is a freeway." Jack was talking excitedly with our friends but I sat still, nestled into that back seat, wide-eyed at the world outside my window but with a little disillusionment creeping into my mind. I had thought that California would be a wonderland, but there were gas stations, fast food restaurants, tracks of homes, road signs — just as we had at home. As I contemplated this situation, suddenly I sensed the Lord speaking to my heart. "Mary Jean, it doesn't matter where you are or what you have. What matters is what you do with where you are and what you have."

That was a valuable lesson.

The important thing is to learn all we can about the Lord right where we are and let Him and His power flow through us to those around us. We can always love and encourage and help regardless of the position we find ourselves in.

When Jack and I launched West Houston Christian Center, I became disoriented trying to figure out my place as the wife of a senior pastor. God in His faithfulness taught me another simple truth: Every position has value. We can be the person making decisions, or the one helping the decision-maker, and both jobs are important.

Jesus came into the world in a stable and was laid in a manger. God Himself, in human form, found Himself lying in a feeding trough! That reminds me of where we find ourselves sometimes. We may have to sacrifice our desires to be obedient to God's will and to hold the position He gives us. But God does not take nearly as much pleasure in our sacrifices as He does in our obedience.[36] Regardless of what we may have to give up in order to serve the Lord, the important issue is not how much we lose, but how obedient we are to Him.

How great it would be for each of us to adopt as our prayer a verse like, "I come . . . to do thy will, O God."[37]

If we truly are living to please God, if we trust that He will work only good for us when we do His will, then we can humble ourselves to obey no matter what He asks us to do.

To learn to submit, we need to make our heart's cry the desire to be like Jesus.

- We are called out from doing things in the way the world does them.

- In His submission to the Cross, Jesus broke the power of the devil over us for all eternity.

- Whether male or female, when we submit to God we align ourselves with Christ and release God's power into our lives.

- In our weakest moment, God's power is perfected in us and made strong on our behalf.

- As we put ourselves into the seemingly weak position of submission, we qualify for the release of God's power in and through us.

- The vast difference between man-preached submission and God-intended submission is that one is a suppressive bondage and the other is a release of the miracle-working power of God.

111

- As we highlight the good in others, we will see great qualities emerge from them.

- Submitting to God through another person shows a greater measure of faith than submitting to God directly.

- Many men are poor leaders because they have not learned to become good helpers. When the woman learns her role and reflects the helper image to the man, he can learn what truly helps.

- We can be the person making decisions, or the one helping the decision-maker, and both jobs are important.

- It doesn't matter where you are or what you have, but what you do with where you are and what you have.

Chapter 8

From Womb to Tomb: Don't Change the Guard

Autumne and I were chatting in the church lobby after services when her ten-year-old son ran up to hand her his Sunday School papers.

"Hi, Toby!" I said.

He mumbled something unintelligible before Autumne rescued him.

"Toby just finished baseball season," she said proudly, smiling down approvingly at her son. "His team went all the way through the playoffs and missed the championship round by only one game."

"Well, that's great, Toby," I said. "We're so proud of you."

Ten-year-olds can't stand too much praise so he quickly escaped us to play with his friends. When he was out of earshot, Autumne winked at me and said, "Thank goodness his team didn't make it!"

"Why?" I asked as her comment took me by surprise.

"Are you kidding?" she said with a giggle. "Six more weeks of car pools, sweaty children and dirty uniforms? Let the other team's mothers deal with it — I'm free!"

I could understand her point. After all, what mother

113

really wants six additional weeks of mending bruised bodies and feelings, chauffeuring noisy little athletes and battling grass stains? For that matter, what woman wants to change diapers, start yet another load of laundry or sit through another Parents Night at school? Who wants to take a camping vacation only to use primitive laundromats, monitor arguments in the back seat and make campfire dinners with their cold water clean-up?

Mothering could put a strain on a worker ant, yet mothers just keep on, one child after another, year after year, in what seems like an unceasing lifestyle. Then one day the children are grown and gone and the child-rearing stage of life that Mom has grown so accustomed to is abruptly over. Suddenly those strained memories take on a certain sweetness and humor.

Many women would like to go back and do their child-rearing over for different reasons. My basic flaw was that I failed really to enjoy my children during those hectic days, mostly because I was uneducated in the mother's most important purpose. Like Autumne, I was caught up in Little League, birthdays, fund-raisers and volunteering for everything. I remember my mother-in-law trying to tell me that when the little boys were grown and gone, I would find myself missing those days. Instead of heeding her advice, I thought, "She doesn't know what I'm going through! I'll be *glad* when they're grown!"

Just before Charlie turned eighteen, I was dusting his picture one day and thought, "Well, this is almost over." I thought that the load of responsibility would soon be off my shoulders. Immediately I sensed the Lord trying to correct me but I couldn't understand, so I tucked the thoughts into the back of my mind.

A few weeks later my mother called after talking to my older sister who had been having some problems.

"Well, I think we've got things straightened out for now," my mom said with a sigh. "I tell you, kids are from the womb to the tomb."

My mind ignited with what was wrong with my comment days earlier. *From the womb to the tomb!* I suddenly realized that I would never outgrow the position of "mother." I would care for my Charlie forever.

There is far more to child-rearing than the early years of diapers, dirty clothes and driving. When children are small, we have undisputed control over them. But when they get older and develop a strong will of their own, we have to decide when to let them go and when to hold them back. My children came into the world without benefit of the good Christian teaching we have today. By the time they entered their teens, I was just learning how to walk in God's grace as a parent. With years of damage behind us, it was difficult to change myself, and nearly impossible to change them.

When Charlie finally left home, I cried in sheer relief because he had been so horribly difficult to raise. But those tears were only for a day. Weeks later I cried for the loss of him, and a season of life whose passing brought deep unsettling. I cried for the unresolved feelings left from butting heads so often. I cried for him because ours was the only mother-son relationship he knew, and it was less than ideal. And I cried in regret because I had not capitalized on the season while I was in it.

I truly regret that I did not learn my position in the home sooner. I had tried to use my power in the physical realm and had bred resentment in my entire family when I was wrong or overbearing. Before the last of the three boys left, I finally realized where a mother's real power lies.

The Bible admonishes us "older" women to "teach the young women to be sober, to love their husbands, to love their children."[1]

I now understand the need to *learn* to love our husbands and children. Generally speaking, we automatically love husbands and children emotionally, but we must learn to love them in action. One avenue of love is to take up the position of a guard.

In Scripture, women are called "to be sensible, pure, workers at home, kind, . . . subject to their own husbands, that the word of God may not be dishonored."[2] The term "workers at home" literally means "stayers at home" or "guards."

Would anyone leave a fort or military installation unprotected? No. He would hire sensible, self-controlled guards to keep it safe. Husbands and wives together are shepherds of their child's soul. Men have been given guardianship as part of their role, but women also have a critical part to play in the protection of their offspring. I don't intend to diminish or demean the man's role, but rather to identify the woman's position, isolate it for clarification, then discuss her power in it.

Women are sensitive to the hidden matters of the heart and innately designed to be protectors of the unseen world. A woman's duty in the family can be summarized as the spiritual guard of both heart and hearth. Just as a hired sentry can see physical trouble coming and take steps to prevent it, women are uniquely created to sense spiritual trouble when it comes near and to ward it off. They are to guard the hearts of their families "with all diligence" for out of the heart spring the issues and forces of life.[3]

Once I accepted the position of guarding my family, many times I sensed a need in one of my boys. In talking with and teaching others, I have found that when a mother is paying attention she can usually pick up attitudes in her children. Sometimes a child may just need encouragement or someone to talk to. If the parent is not available or does not show interest, these are the times the child will go elsewhere and perhaps receive poor counsel from a peer or some other influence. Other times children can make new friends who are not a good influence on them. An attentive mother can perceive these matters and take them to the Lord in prayer.

Raising three boys, I especially learned to watch over the female relationships in their lives. I specifically asked God to protect my sons and to turn them away from the influence of adulterous women. Having knowledge of this subject made me well aware of how a woman can influence a man, even a young man, for good or evil. In our present day, young girls are becoming promiscuous even as pre-teens. Mothers of daughters have a specific responsibility to guard them in prayer, as do mothers of sons.

We mothers actually operate on two levels. We fight for our children spiritually and discipline their flesh physically. We are not to fight with them physically and discipline them spiritually. Since the physical realm follows the spiritual, the woman sets the atmosphere of her home through the influence of her spirit more than through physical management. The two operating together keep her children from harm. Of the two, the spirit is most often overlooked, yet greater spiritual warfare results in fewer physical fights.

I had to learn to fight for my teenagers spiritually, and not with them physically. There is a very subtle difference between the two, and the self-discipline involved can be trying. But wrangling back and forth with our kids is far worse, as it chips away at us without our even realizing it. In their teens, children push at the boundaries as hard as they do in earlier years and maybe even harder. They need the security of knowing that Mom (and Dad ideally) is still there and still cares. As Christian parents, we need to stay spiritually alert.

The Bible states, "'Honor your father and your mother, that your days may be long upon the land which the Lord your God is giving you.'"[4] When children do not honor the words of their parents, they separate themselves from the presence of God and open themselves to evil influences. They need someone to ask for God's mercy and forgiveness for them to open the way for them to come back. I found that in order for me to ask for God's forgiveness for Charlie, I first had to forgive him myself. When he removed the spiritual covering provided by his parents, I had to overlook personal hurt and humiliation and care enough to exercise the power of intercession on his behalf.

One of the penalties for a rebellious son in the Old Testament was to be taken out and stoned to death.[5] This always seemed rather harsh when I would read it as I worked my way through my Bible. But the truth of that Scripture only becomes clear through New Testament terms. The rebellious child has taken on a form of death in his life, not by stoning at the hands of others, but by his own separation from God. Our job as mothers and guardians is to cover the sins of our children by praying for their forgiveness through the blood of Jesus, asking the Lord to open their eyes to the truth.

One day when Charlie was a young teenager we had one of those little eruptions that often start at about that age. (They seem to get better at age sixteen or seventeen, then begin to worsen again when they are eighteen and "know everything.") This one started on what had been a splendid Saturday morning until Charlie announced his decision to go to the beach with a neighbor.

"Mom, Dad," Charlie proclaimed triumphantly as he strode into the living room that morning, "I'm going to the beach with Jason."

"Who's driving?" Jack asked.

"Jason," Charlie answered.

"Since when did Jason start driving?"

"Since yesterday when he got his license."

"And his parents are giving him the car to drive all the way to the beach?" Jack asked. "That's an hour and a half away!"

"Yeah, isn't that great?"

Charlie may as well have asked Jack to let Jason borrow *our* car and to give them each fifty dollars just for the fun of it. I knew I would jump in and confuse the issue if I stayed around, so I stole away to the comparative isolation of the next room.

Jack's style of parenting drove me crazy. Like the time I tried to return to the house after taking a walk and found myself locked out. When I looked through the window, there were two of my sons in a fist fight with Jack looking on. The boys were about six and eight and Jack was fed up with their constant bickering and tattling, so he was letting them fight it out. When I tried to insist he let me in, he said no, it was better I stay out and let them finish. I should have known then that Jack and I would have different parenting styles for life.

Years later I finally gave up trying to correct Jack, which didn't work anyway, and on this day I needed to get into position silently to influence the storm that was brewing. From the dining room I could hear the conversation continue and their voices rise a little.

"Well, first of all you can start asking instead of announcing your plans," Jack said. "And secondly, you're not going to the beach alone with just another kid, especially one who doesn't know anything about driving."

"Right, Dad," came the sarcastic and angry retort. "They just gave Jason his license because he doesn't know anything about driving."

I unconsciously grabbed hold of the back of a chair, perhaps to stop myself from rushing back into the room to tell Charlie off. In the swell of emotions, I bowed my head and began to pray for God to move in a way that would lift the name of Jesus; to forgive me, Charlie, Jack and all concerned; to give Jack wisdom and to open Charlie's eyes to truth. When I finished praying, Charlie had stormed upstairs to his room and Jack was sitting undisturbed in the den. I decided that this was the right time to run an errand I had put off earlier.

Alone in the peaceful quiet of my car, I continued to pray over the situation. When I returned about an hour later, Jack was still in his chair and Charlie was still in his room. I went about my business when suddenly I heard Charlie walking slowly down the stairs. He made his way over to Jack and I fell in behind him to see what was going to happen.

"Dad, I'm sorry," Charlie said. When Jack looked up from his book I could see his calm, fatherly expression. "I really didn't want to go anyway."

"Then why did you put us through all that?" Jack asked.

"I don't know. I just felt like I had to."

Typical teenager. Charlie was pushing, but really just wanted the assurance that the boundaries were still there. We show love to our children by giving them those boundaries and not blowing up at them every time they test one. This was a living example for me. It was one of the first times I had done the right thing and handled the situation in the spirit realm. The result was far better than any I could have achieved by getting involved in the physical realm, and a peaceful home was the reward.

Against all the other activities of motherhood, praying for our children is the most important. No one else will care for them as much as we do, regardless of how often our friends or relatives pray for them. Children won't just automatically make the decisions and follow the lifestyle we and the Lord want them to. They have to be prayed into it. When we take our position as a guard, God's power will flow through us to bring our children to the place He has designed for them.

Jesus has made provision for us in watching over our households:

- We have the blood of Jesus that cleanses us from sin.[6]

- We have the name of Jesus that carries His authority.[7]

- We have the Word of God that moves the spirit realm.[8]

These are the "weapons" of our position as guards.[9] Keep your house "covered" in the blood of Jesus through prayer. Keep Jesus' name lifted up over your household. And speak the Word of God over your household and all who are in it every day.

The Word of God contains powerful prayers with which we can guard our families. One of the first Scriptures I learned to pray over my family was from the first chapter of the Book of Ephesians (Ephesians 1:17-20). Later I found Proverbs to be a great source for answers. There are thirty-one chapters in Proverbs, one for each day of the month. The first chapter says that the proverbs bring understanding, so it is a good exercise to read one chapter a day. Often I begin my quiet time by reading the proverb of the day and God often speaks to me through it about a specific situation I am in or praying about.

One day recently I set aside a morning just to pray for my sons. I talked to the Lord about them and read my Bible seeking wisdom as to how to pray more. A knock at the door startled me out of my devotions. It was Charlie. He came by the house because an appointment he had scheduled ended early and he wanted to take me to breakfast. As I sat across the table from him at Denny's, I was in awe of how prayer changes things! This was a child who once looked me in the eye and, full of rebellious hatred, said he never wanted to see me again. That morning I stayed calm on the surface, laughing and chatting with him, but inside I soared with the overwhelming sense of the faithfulness of God.

If prayer can work this way with grown children, how much more will it work with small children, especially if a mother is wise enough to start when a child is born.

We will see victories in our family when we stay in the Word, study the Word, and utilize the Word in prayer. Acting on God's Word will see us through any crisis.

Jack and I went through a particularly difficult crisis when Charlie was fourteen and suddenly started to swell inexplicably all over his body. I thought he was gaining weight at first until I realized that it was not fat, but swollen flesh I saw bulging beneath his clothes. We rushed him to the doctor who began a series of tests.

Jack and I were faithful churchgoers by this time, but still did not understand the divine order of God in our home. I had learned that Jack was ultimately responsible in God's eyes as "head" of the family, and had swung from one end of the pendulum to the other. Instead of taking everything away from Jack and usurping his authority as I had in the past, I was now dumping everything into his lap, whether he was ready for it or not. I had learned just enough to be dangerous.

"Why isn't Jack taking his spiritual place as leader in this crisis?" I complained to God one night in prayer. "He's not doing a single thing to help anyone, and Charlie is only getting worse!"

That night I heard the Lord saying to my heart that if I was the one who could see the problem, I was the one who needed to pray over it. God would not absolve me of personal responsibility even though He required Jack to be the head of our home. I began to pray differently from that point on.

If the woman discerns a problem, it is her responsibility to take action on it in prayer, whether others see it or not.

Sometimes we use the verse "there is neither male nor female" only when it works in our favor.[10]

My mistake was in expecting Jack to see things exactly as I did, and to lead us in prayer together. I started into the crisis doing the worst thing I could have done — getting angry with my husband for not being "spiritually attuned" to the same things I was.

When the Lord showed me my position as guard for my family, I placed myself where His power could flow through me, regardless of what Jack did. Charlie was soon diagnosed with a kidney disease, so at least the waiting was over and treatment would begin. As we continued to stand our ground spiritually, he was healed and has enjoyed good health ever since.

When we have a crisis, whether illness or anything else, if we take our position, God's power will flow through us into that crisis.

Proverbs 31 is the "virtuous woman" chapter of the Bible from which hundreds of studies have sprung. In it, we read that the "virtuous woman" rises from bed while it is still dark to care for her family.[11] I believe this is an allegory in physical terms of what we women do spiritually. We rise up in the midst of darkness and pray for God to bring His power into the situation and circumstances of our lives. The virtuous woman is also said to "clothe" her family,[12] which I believe refers to the spiritual covering our prayers provide over them. Elsewhere in Scripture we see that even if a person, perhaps a son or daughter, tries to hide from God in darkness, God's light will penetrate that darkness and come to that individual.[13] We can bring God's light to our children regardless of where they are, what circumstances they are in, how old they have grown.

Today my sons are well into their twenties and none of them has married. Now my prayers for them are different. I pray for God to give them His choice in a wife. I ask God specifically to send someone who will continue the years of prayer I have already built up, not someone who will tear down what God has established within their precious lives. I refer to their future wives as Ruth, Abigail and Esther. I would be happy with one of each, but what I ask the Lord for is to give each of their wives the strengths of all of these women. Ruth had a faithful, persevering spirit (and loved her mother-in-law as well).[14] Abigail was an intercessor for her husband even though he was a fool.[15] Esther had a humble, submissive and graceful quality about her (and was the most beautiful woman in the land, which of course my sons would like).[16] This is a lot to ask for, yet the Apostle Paul says that our God is able to do even more than we can ask or even think.[17]

When a woman like me has stepchildren or has remarried and created a stepfather to her children, I believe the responsibilities remain the same. It doesn't work for a woman to live with a child under her roof who doesn't fall under her authority and influence. It is critical for the stepparent to stand in agreement with the spouse, and vice versa, as to the spiritual and physical welfare of the child. Years ago when I became pregnant with Jack's child, we went to court to adopt each other's children. A chill ran through me when the judge looked sternly over the top of his glasses at me and said, "Young lady, are you willing to give up half your rights to your child's discipline?" I had hardly caught my breath when he looked at Jack and said, "Young man, are you willing to support this child until he is eighteen, whether this marriage works out or not?"

This was the best counsel we could have received, as it heightened our awareness of the gravity of our actions. I have seen many marriages dissolve because the natural parent could not give any rights to the stepparent, or the stepparent would not accept any responsibilities for the stepchild. The answer is always adoption, though not necessarily legal adoption. If a child is under your roof, you have the right and responsibility to exercise your God-given gifts on behalf of that child. Couples need to agree together on the physical discipline and spiritual welfare of every child in the family to keep from falling into discord.

Regardless of the age of your children, your relationship to them or their place in life today, I challenge you to take your position as a guard. If your husband is agreeable to stand with you in this position, invite him to join you.

I believe that God will ask us mothers two questions when we see Him in eternity. The first is, "What did you do with My Son, Jesus?" We will answer that we believed on Him for salvation. The second is, "What did you do with those whom I entrusted to you?" And that is the answer we are still forming.

Our husbands, children and even grandchildren are the primary recipients of our influence. They must always be our priority. Next to them comes the lives of our extended family, church, ministry, work and other friends whom God has brought into our lives.

Has someone else taken the place of your children in your prayers?

Let go of the hurt, anger, disappointment, resentment or even sentiment. Your children need Jesus! If they win the Nobel Prize, or achieve the height of glory in their vocation, but don't know the Lord, they still desperately need your prayers because *they need Jesus.*

- Children are from the womb to the tomb.

- A woman's duty is to be the spiritual guard of both heart and hearth.

- Fight for your teenagers spiritually, not with them physically.

- We will see victories in our family when we stay in the Word, study the Word and utilize the Word in prayer.

- If the woman discerns a problem, it is her responsibility to take action on it in prayer, whether others see it or not.

- When we have a crisis, such as illness, and take our position, God's power will flow through us into that crisis.

- Regardless of the age of your children or how far they have drifted, you can still maintain your position as guard and release God's power in their lives.

Chapter 9

The Balance of Responsibilities

Crazy, but statistics indicate that women who work outside the home put in almost as many hours working in the home as those who don't have an outside job. For some reason, we accept this as the modern woman's job description: earn the money that buys the food, shop for the food, balance the checkbook that bought the food, cook the food, clean up after serving the food, and go back to work the next day to earn more money to buy more food. This certainly doesn't sound like progress, does it?

For years I struggled internally about going to work outside the home. When my children were small, our society was in a different mode. Women were burning their bras, unappreciated wives and mothers were running away from home, and working women were challenging the male-dominated establishment. Women who stayed at home, à la Donna Reed, were considered to have less intelligence, as if they were home because they were incapable of doing anything else. Staying home was simply out of style. In those days, I was a member of the unpopular stay-at-home crowd, and it rankled me to be called a woman who "did not work." I remember once at a beauty shop the young woman shampooing my hair asked, "Do you work out of the home or in the home?" Her words were like a refreshing drink as she acknowledged that, for a woman, staying home was still work. Is it ever!

Much of my time during those years was spent in organizing school carnivals, running Little League concession stands, attending room mothers' meetings, cooking and serving at spaghetti dinners and in many other such non-paying endeavors. My friends laughingly observed that I volunteered half my life away. But when I paused long enough to reflect on my many and varied activities, I often yearned for another type of work, something with a reward to it. The volunteer jobs would end and I longed for a paycheck, or some morale booster to encourage me, but there was nothing except the next fund-raiser, team playoff or homeroom party.

Motherhood demands the most devotion, extracts the longest hours, allows the fewest days off, provides the worst vacation policy and pays the lowest wages of any job known to humanity. Of course, parenting contributes the most benefits to humanity, but there are times when we lose sight of that fact.

I remember one particularly low moment when I was driving to Bible study and complaining to God because I didn't have a job outside the home. I suppose I was assuming that He wasn't even listening when suddenly a thought popped into my mind, as if God had spoken directly to my heart saying, *Why do you want a job?*

At first I was startled, then I plunged in, thinking of all the benefits that work would give me. I could almost hear the whine in my thoughts as if I were speaking aloud. "I want to be able to dress up and go someplace; I want people to tell me I look nice and that I'm doing a good job; and I want to get a paycheck for all my hard work."

These reasons came quickly off the top of my head, but when I paused to think of others, another thought suddenly occurred to me. *All my "reasons" were just ways to feed my pride.* A little taken aback but stubborn as I am, I plunged in again, this time coming up with as unselfish a reason as I could muster. "Well, not just that, but I want to help our household with the money situation," I thought self-righteously.

Once again the Lord convicted me. *I was accusing Him of not taking care of my family properly, and I did not have an attitude of appreciation.* This whole mental process was getting deep, and my mind was in a skid, looking for some way to justify myself.

When I let go of the train of thought, I was left with the shameful realization that my fretting stemmed from two attributes — pride and fear — that wouldn't get me any place I wanted to go. God had nailed me where it hurt most — the motivation of my heart.

As it turned out, I did not work outside the home until the children were much older, and I can now see the Lord's wisdom in holding me back. It was as much for Him to train me as it was for me to train them.

Other women have far different experiences and convictions. I don't believe there is one hard-and-fast mandate from God in this area, and for every rule we made we could possibly find a million exceptions, but I do believe these three things:

One: The world pressures women to be out of the home. This was certainly true in my case. So many alluring things are offered, so many enticing roads beckon, so much condemnation is encountered by the woman who decides "just" to stay home. Today, we wives are almost programmed to believe that we hold no value unless we are contributing to the physical provision of the household. It seems that we are almost blind to the far more valuable yet intangible influences we contribute.

Two: Some women are called of God into a work situation to be His influence there. Every circumstance holds more opportunity than what meets the eye. I believe some women are literally called by God almost as missionaries into certain environments, occupying a spiritual position while fulfilling a physical need. I am certainly not one to condemn working women; however, the next point presents the "flip side" of this coin.

Three: Many women have gone to work for the wrong reasons. Just as I discovered the pride and fear in my heart, all women would do well to examine honestly their own personal motivation for wanting to get out of the house and a get a paying job. Many are too impatient to wait for God to work things out in their husband's situation, and so they take things into their own hands. Some are just greedy. Others are blind to the welfare of their children.

As women, we are created to be in relationship with a man as his helper. When we try to "help" the man by stepping into his role and infringing on his area of authority, we are not helping but hindering him in the development of his manhood. A woman who openly "rescues" her husband — or publicly "steps on his toes," perhaps by second-guessing him in front of his staff or by vying for a volunteer position alongside him — is a source of embarrassment to the man and creates an uncomfortably awkward situation for all concerned.

Learning to step aside from, instead of stepping into, a husband's role, can be a difficult lesson to master, but is important for the development of both parties. In my case, the Lord's plan for Jack was to provide for his household, under the direction of God Who is ultimately our Provider. I had to let Jack work this situation out with the Lord himself. This decision became my way of helping in that my absence allowed Jack an opportunity to grow in relationship to his God.

The Lord drew me up short some years after the struggle I mentioned previously, but this time in a different way. Jack was struggling with a business deal and suddenly I found myself in the position of a "Jezebel." In the biblical account of Ahab, his wife Jezebel was a wicked Baal-worshipper and the princess of a heathen nation. Although Ahab was king over God's people, he aligned himself through marriage with a wicked woman who incited him to do all sorts of evil and who eventually usurped his authority completely. At one point, Ahab came home complaining that he couldn't have a field he wanted because it belonged by ancestral rights to another man. Jezebel was disgusted at her husband for whining instead of taking action, so she sent out her henchmen to kill the owner of the field and transfer title over to the king. Ultimately, both she and Ahab paid the price for their wickedness with their lives.

Jezebel is not the only woman who was ever tempted to interfere in her husband's dealings. Jack had come home from work frustrated one day. We were standing in the kitchen having a snack late that afternoon when he unburdened all the gory details of a business deal in which he felt he was being cheated by another individual. While I listened, I felt red-hot anger well up inside me. How dare that man treat my husband that way! I was about to speak my mind and tell Jack exactly what to do, when the Lord showed me my own heart. It was as if suddenly I heard my voice saying, "Me Jezebel. You Ahab. I'll get that field for you, Baby!"

While Jack continued talking, I wrestled myself down inside. This business deal was not my business deal; it was Jack's. As his helper, I was called to counsel him, pray for and with him and to love him through this situation, but I was never asked by him or God or anyone else to do the work for him. I believed the situation warranted direct confrontation with this man and struggled not to blurt out, "Jack, get out there and fight like a man!" Instead, I waited my turn to speak and then offered counsel.

"Well, maybe you should talk to him," I suggested.

"No, I need to wait it out," Jack answered.

I bit my tongue to keep from saying more. The truth is, I was sure I was right. Later, when I was alone and could pray about it, I submitted the situation to the Lord for Him to work it out for the best. Even then, I felt certain that God was going to tell Jack to confront the man, just as I had suggested.

Instead, quite a different thing happened. As Jack continued to wait for things to change, and I continued to press on in prayer, God took over the situation in a most supernatural, miraculous way. The business deal came to a close in such a way that without doing a thing, Jack wasn't cheated. God revealed Himself as the Creator God Who has endless ways to achieve His ends, once situations are put into His Hands.

As the old saying goes, "There is more than one way to skin a cat." When dealing with an infinite God, this is definitely true. With His limitless creative power, God can take even negatives and transform them into positives.

And, if we allow Him, He will do it in a way that fits our individual personalities.

The result of that episode was that Jack and I both grew in faith. When it was all over, we were not only still married, we were still friends.

This was an extremely tough, but important lesson for me in learning the role of the female. As we move in and out of these roles of authority and influence, we as women will face similar situations to Jack's. We will be in the position of authority when someone who is supposed to be a helper gets involved in our business and muddles things up. I can think of many times this has happened to me in volunteer work. In the position of authority, we learn to trust in God for direction and in overcoming obstacles. In the position of influence, we learn to trust God through another person, which is more difficult.

Women, particularly strong and capable women, get into trouble in their marriages and other relationships because of misdirected "help." When in the female role, we are called to help others do the work, not do the work for them. As wives whose husbands are struggling to make a living, or as mothers whose children are grappling with a decision, sometimes the best thing we can do for them is pray and support them, but allow them to discover their own solutions.

A friend was working on her master's degree when she married an x-ray technician. His paltry salary barely kept them alive until her graduation, by which time she was pregnant. Instead of pursuing a career, she believed God wanted her to stay home to raise their newborn child. She learned to manage with the inconveniences of one car, a one-bedroom apartment and little money. Later another company moved into their area and needed technicians. She encouraged and prayed for her husband, giving him the confidence to sail through the interviews and land the job, which doubled his income. Two more babies came, but the couple still couldn't move out of the tiny, cramped apartment. Then another job opportunity came up, and again she encouraged her husband. Again he landed it. Since their marriage, his income has quadrupled and they are now building their own home. She could have taken a job to achieve the same external results sooner, but the internal results may never have come. In waiting on God to work things out with her husband, she "helped" him become more of a man.

I realize that some women believe they have almost a "divine right" not to work simply by virtue of being born female. I have heard of women who wanted to walk out on their marriages just because a husband asked for help in his growing business. This attitude is neither submissive nor mature, and it is certainly not the attitude of a "helper." There are seasons in life, and when the season comes, we have to flow with it. The important thing to know is what God is saying to do at a given moment. If you do end up helping your husband at his work, remember that you are his helper, not his boss.

If a man is to develop in his maleness and as a leader, which is God's purpose for man, then he needs someone whom he can lead. If you are his wife, that "someone" is you. It is difficult for some women to let someone else lead and provide for them, and yet this is God's plan in order to develop each person involved. Praying for our husbands and believing God will enable them to do what is right creates greater trust in God. Trusting the Lord matures and perfects us. We must trust God far more when we are trusting Him in another person rather than in ourselves.

Many times we are tempted to do something ourselves rather than to wait on the man to develop in that area. Other times we simply let our physical desires get the best of us. Some women go to work merely because of greed. They want more, and their husbands aren't giving it to them. Instead of adjusting their lifestyle and waiting for God to work things out in the husband's career, these women try to do it on their own.

The well-intentioned but poorly-motivated co-provider can open the door for many evils. The man can become lazy, wanting to fall back since the woman is picking up the slack. Or he can become inhibited, particularly if the woman's success becomes greater than his own. In his discouragement, he may fail to keep trying or giving his best, which thwarts God's purposes for his life. The man can even become fearful for his wife to quit work, unwilling to shoulder the load alone since he has become accustomed to her help in carrying it. This situation can create resentment in his wife because he demands that she work, while perhaps she feels the tug to stay home.

At this point, the working wife is no longer a helper, but has become a crutch. By encroaching on the husband's position, a woman actually feeds his weaknesses and denies him the opportunity to develop his strengths.

As loving wives, the idea that we may be hindering instead of helping our husbands is tough on our pride when we realize we are wrong. But God's Spirit brings conviction, not condemnation.

It is important to realize that the man who feels responsible for his family will develop far more in his spirit than the man whose God-given responsibility has been diluted or diverted. As the woman prays for and influences her husband, he will feel the pressures of his responsibility which he cannot bear alone, see the opportunity to turn to God and discover that the Lord is always there for him. Thus the woman in both prayer and action helps "birth" the man spiritually.

Through conviction and repentance we are set free. When God releases us from the pressures and images of this world, we are released from the bondage of sin and set free to become all He created us to be.

Concerning work outside the home, we need to see it in relation to husbands, and as mothers. Many good books and teaching abound on this subject, so let's get right to the point. Children need parents! It is a well-documented, commonly understood fact that the more time a mother can give her child, the better off that child will be. When the mother influences the child for Christ, the value of her time is infinitely compounded. The mother who uses her power of influence to affect her own offspring in essence affects hundreds more by mere association as the years roll by.

I would rather minister the Gospel of Jesus Christ to one person who receives it than to head the largest corporation in the country without influencing a single life for eternity. If we can do both, and have a positive impact on hundreds of lives, great. But if we win the world and lose our own families, we fail in our purpose.[1] The scope of the power in ministering the life-giving truth of Jesus Christ cannot be overstated. Our families are to be the primary recipients of our ministry.

Mindy is a capable young woman in one of my Bible studies whose career as an engineer took off. The money was great, her self-esteem was at an all-time high, she looked and dressed like the successful woman she was, her husband openly adored her and everyone wanted to be her friend. Life was sweet! Then she got pregnant.

"Mary Jean, I want to be a good mother," she confided in me one day after our study, "but my career won't wait. If I take time off, the technology will change and I'll never be able to get back into the field."

I prayed with her, then counseled, "Mindy, don't try to make that decision today. Just relax and enjoy being pregnant, then let God make clear what you should do."

"But I can't accept that," she countered. "I don't know what to tell my boss — if I should resign completely or just take maternity leave — and it's eating me up."

"God's plan for you will unfold," I assured her.

Mindy slowly unwound and, without a definite answer from the Lord, she took maternity leave. Once little Tabatha was born and Mindy was home with her twenty-four hours a day, she grew stir-crazy. Preparing bottles, changing diapers, going through the same routine time and again was no match for the exciting projects that captivated her imagination and utilized her high-tech training at work. Mindy was thrilled five months later when she dropped off little Tabatha at daycare and returned to work.

She came to Bible study in a state of exhilaration. "I'm so happy, I still have my job and my baby, too!" she said. "It's all working out great."

Everything was fine for a few months, then she started worrying aloud once again. "I miss my baby so much," she told us. "This seemed like such a great opportunity. But I can't shake my desire to be with Tabatha, dirty diapers and all."

We prayed with her and she went home to tell her husband of her concern. At first he was worried about the possibility of living without her income, but he agreed to pray about it. Weeks passed until one morning Mindy had a revelation. As she was getting dressed for work and choosing an outfit for Tabatha, she thought, "I would never let anyone else choose Tabatha's clothes."

Looking around the room she thought, "I would never let anyone decorate her nursery . . . or my house . . . or choose my clothes . . . or decide my hairstyle." Then the thunderbolt hit. "And yet, I'm letting someone else decide how to raise my daughter."

She picked up Tabatha and raced to the other room where her husband was getting ready for work. They prayed together, and she decided to resign. They are now in the process of changing their lifestyle so they can live on one income and, as I write, last Thursday was her last day on the job. I believe God has a ministry for Mindy that will fulfill her in a way she doesn't yet realize exists.

This is an ideal situation, in which a husband and wife are both in the home and agree on the training of the children. But even when circumstances fall short of the "ideal," God will work things out for the woman who seeks Him and places herself in a position that honors Him. So often we blindly press on in the physical realm, trying to do everything "right" yet without evaluating the position in which we find ourselves.

Jesus taught us to pray "deliver us from evil."[2] Another reading is, "deliver us from our own laborious effort."[3]

Sometimes we need to be delivered from ourselves.

Many mothers like Mindy stay home for a brief time then take an outside job as the child grows older. We seem to accept as fact that our children don't need us as much in their teen years as they do when they are small. Yet if we take an honest look at the state of teenagers today, we can see for ourselves that this assumption does not hold true. Psychologist James Dobson wrote, "How often have you heard some mothers of little ones say, 'I don't plan to work until the kids are in kindergarten.' . . . In reality, the teen years will generate as much pressure on them as the preschool years — and more!"[4]

Children at all ages need mothers to be available to mother them.

The turmoil in our world creates an even greater need for us to be in a position to influence our children. When my children were teenagers I learned that I had to concentrate on them and ask the right questions. They didn't want to share themselves with me, so I had to dedicate myself to keep the communication flowing, which required a lot of time. I learned to capitalize on each moment I found alone with one of them to communicate more deeply. Finding such moments is difficult when working full time elsewhere.

Working outside the home is even more difficult when raising children who have special problems. Besides physical disabilities, there are those with emotional impairments who need more direct care and nurture. Charlie was a textbook case of a divorce victim. During his teen years we experienced many difficulties directly tied to the divorce many years earlier. Even though our relationships were good with our ex-spouses, our children had been shaken in their foundations, and we had to deal with it. This kind of work is not something to be palmed off onto counselors, daycare workers, coaches or teachers. Children need parents first, then all the other adults in their network of support.

Women can work outside the home, but many are working for the wrong reasons, and many are inadvertently hindering their husbands and children. Working to ensure that children and husbands have a relationship with God results in eternal significance and should not be labeled as unimportant or less vital than other work. In fact, it is the most crucial work a wife and mother can do.

Now for the other side of the coin. Some women must work outside the home, and others know God has sent them to a specific situation for a specific purpose of evangelism, ministry or other influence. We must always be "prioritizing our activities" and "discerning the seasons" in the lives of our loved ones. Why should my family miss God's blessing while I reach out to bless others? This is a question for the career woman as well as the woman who volunteers her life away as I once did.

Years after I settled my internal struggle about working outside the home, God led me to take a temporary position. What a switch! By this time, I knew I wanted to be in full-time ministry to the Lord, working side by side with my husband, yet I was impelled to go out into the secular labor force for which I had yearned years earlier, but whose luster had dimmed considerably. God used the time to take us through the transition from Jack's business life to the beginning of his full-time ministry. By working, I paid the price along with Jack for the calling of God on our lives. I can see the wisdom of God in it now although it was a difficult and humbling season of life.

If you find yourself in a position in which you work outside the home, perhaps leaving your children with others and your husband in God's care, be assured that God's grace will cover you and them in any situation. We long for God's ideal plan while living in an imperfect world with imperfect people. As we position ourselves according to His Word, His power brings our lives into greater and greater alignment with His ideal.

Remember, Jesus fills in all the gaps. He is our righteousness.[5] When we are not able to live the ideal life for reasons beyond our control, He is perfect within us.[6]

- We must trust God far more when we are trusting Him in another person rather than in ourselves.

- By encroaching on her husband's position, a woman actually feeds his weaknesses and denies him the opportunity to develop his strengths.

- God's Spirit brings conviction, not condemnation. Through conviction and repentance we are set free.

- When God releases us from the pressures and images of this world we are released from the bondage of sin and set free to become all He created us to be.

- Children at all ages need mothers to be available to mother them.

- Parenting is not something to be palmed off onto counselors, daycare workers, coaches or

teachers. Children need parents first, then all
the other adults in their network of support.

- When we are not able to live the ideal life for
reasons beyond our control, Jesus is perfect
within us.

Chapter 10

Single and in Place

Single living is so prevalent that most women today can expect to be on their own at some time in their lives. Married women encounter challenges similar to those of single women when their husbands travel extensively, keep odd hours or are absent from the home for any number of physical, emotional or spiritual reasons. We all have something to learn from successful singles.

Ministering to singles for many years has given me an appreciation of their special circumstances and sometimes special needs. Jack and I were driving to a singles retreat once where we were to be the featured speakers. We were each in silent meditation on the task before us when Jack suddenly broke the silence with, "If you were single, forty years old, and had a rebellious teenage son, what would you need most from God?"

"Well, I would need help to get my son under control," I quickly answered. As I contemplated my single friends for a few minutes I thought of something else. "And," I added, "I would need permission to be happy as a single woman."

It is not easy to be single in what is predominately a married person's world, and even less easy to raise children alone. God has promised special grace to those who find themselves in these situations. "Pure religion and undefiled before God and the Father is this, to visit and help and care for the orphans and widows in their affliction."[1]

God has made special provision for single women and mothers, and He acts upon this promise Himself when He is asked. Not only does He provide help and care, the Lord also promises to be "a father of the fatherless," and the husband of the single woman.[2] Just as we would allow a man to be courteous to us or to give us gifts, so we must allow God to step into these roles in our lives and allow Him the room to exercise His ability on our behalf. Once again, getting into position is the key to power.

Leslie was a tall, attractive woman who came to one of our seminars and testified about raising her daughter alone. Her greatest problem for years was in trying to be both mother and father to little Becky. The Lord ministered to her one day that she need not try to assume the role of father to her daughter because that was the position God had promised to fill. Exhausted and emotionally depleted from trying to be two parents, Leslie moved aside and let Him take over. When she released Becky to the Lord, trusting Him to be a father to her, and as she continually interceded for her as a mother, God was faithful to minister to Becky in a deep, powerful way, bringing her into a close relationship with Him.

God can and does reach our children when we ask Him to do so and then step aside to give Him room to work. Once Leslie released Becky, she released herself as well to allow God to be a husband to her. A tremendous time of spiritual growth and renewal came in Leslie's life as a result. Today, Leslie is a well-adjusted, happy and successful single and her daughter Becky is a well-adjusted, happy young woman who attends our church and who considers her mother to be one of her best friends.

When a parent is missing, or simply neglecting his or her responsibilities, God is willing to fill the void. It is imperative that the operative, believing parent or stepparent help the child develop a positive attitude about the absent parent. This helps keep bitterness from creeping in and destroying the child's life. It also helps nurture the part of the child's identity that is wrapped up in the missing parent. If a parent is talked about as being worthless, then a child will absorb that sense of worthlessness. Coming from that same blood, or genes, the child may feel internally that the same worthlessness will be reproduced in himself or herself. Children will learn to forgive their parents, and see the good in them, when their parents model a positive attitude and actively teach it. Harboring anger or bitterness against a child's natural parent will result in conflict between stepparent and child.

When Jack and I were riding along that day, the first thing that popped into my mind was that God is a father to the fatherless. But the second thing is one I have seen single women struggle with everywhere, that God allows and desires them to be happy! Regardless of our situation or circumstance in life, if we will allow Him to do so, the Lord will make us content, give us a mission that fulfills us and complete us in Himself.

An unspoken but prevalent attitude in our society holds that a single woman will not be happy until she finds a husband. We can see this attitude reflected in books, movies and many television shows. Part of the curse from the fall of man was that the woman would have a longing or a desire for her husband.[3] The sin of lust can also be translated into "longing after something." When the New Testament says that Jesus has set us free from the curse of the law, and from the bondage of sin and our flesh, we can believe that Jesus has set us free from that longing, or "lust" for a man.

Some women spend their whole lives longing to be married. Many then spend their whole married lives longing for their husbands to be someone other than who they are. No male can live up to the image of an ideal man that some women build in their minds before marriage. There is nothing wrong with a healthy desire to have a relationship with a man. God's plan for humanity is to be fruitful and multiply, which is the product of marriage. But it becomes wrong when women cannot act independently of this desire or obey God for fear of not fulfilling their longing. This can become idolatry and is a real snare. Women can fall prey to lies like the story line of *Beauty and the Beast* that they will one day marry, live in a palace with a prince and never have another problem. But the truth is, marriage will not satisfy an unhappy person. Contentment in any and every situation of life is the key to real happiness and fulfillment.[4]

I believe a healthy, fruitful life is available to *every* single woman by serving the Lord wholeheartedly. It is easier to focus on serving Him without the distractions of a husband.[5] The male-female roles are constantly interchanging and flexing as men and women go about their daily business and can be fulfilled any number of ways. A completeness truly does come in marriage when the uniquely designed female complements the uniquely designed male, but single people can find completeness without a spouse. The Apostle Paul tells us that "in him [Jesus] dwelleth all the fulness of the Godhead bodily. And *ye are complete in him.*"[6] Jesus completes by filling the gaps Himself; directing, protecting and providing for the single woman; walking alongside, comforting and encouraging the single man.

Whatever your state, you have permission and provision from the Father to be productive, content and complete. The Apostle Paul even *encouraged* single living, saying that it was good for unmarrieds and widows to stay single as he was.[7]

I doubt that there are many people who get married with a full understanding of all the responsibilities and consequences involved. In a marriage ceremony, the woman vows before God that she will allow the man to lead her through life and be the "helmsman" of their ship, so to speak. That is not something to which one can say "Kings X" or "Oops, I made a mistake" or "I was just kidding." It is not a casual promise that can be easily broken without long-lasting and far-reaching consequences. In that same ceremony, the man vows to protect and provide for the woman *for life* and to receive God's wisdom through her. Suddenly, both are in position to rely on and receive from God through each other, instead of relying on and receiving from God completely on their own as they did in their single days.

One advantage of single living is the freedom to serve the Lord and help others with the whole heart. Such focus and time are not available when a partner is involved. As a single living in a silent apartment, you may miss the comforting sounds of home, but you are free from the distractions of someone knocking at your door demanding something of you every time you start to pray. You may enjoy the late hours you are able to keep when you're single, or you may have trouble filling them, but you are free from the tremendous pressures on your time that come when you have children to raise and a spouse with a different schedule. Every stage of life holds advantages and disadvantages. Use your time! Use your silence! Use your opportunity for productivity and growth!

As a creature whose purpose is to help the man, don't limit your influence and service to the man who was or is to be your husband. Plenty of people in the male role need your help. Deborah is a great example of a woman whose influence on a man who was not her husband helped shape her nation and change history.

Deborah was a married woman who, as a prophetess, became a judge in Israel.[8] Her reputation as a woman who was attuned to the Lord attracted people from all over, both men and women, who flocked to her for all their needs.[9] One day Deborah sent for an army general named Barak, for whom she had a message. In the original Bible language, the connotation is that she literally stretched out to reach him, and prepared herself to preach to him. She wanted to give him a prophecy that would stir up within him the call of God on his life. When he came to her, she started with, "Hath not the Lord God of Israel commanded . . ."[10] This caught Barak's attention! Then she told him to go into battle on behalf of Israel. Barak must have realized that this was the voice of the Lord, but he responded in a strange way.

"If you will go with me, then I will go," Barak said, "but if you will not go with me, I will not go."[11]

When I used to read this response as a young Christian, I thought Barak was reluctant to fight and therefore pretty wimpy. Now I realize how powerful a statement this was. What courage it took for a man of war to admit his need of a woman, especially in that day when the prevailing philosophers had poisoned the minds of men against women. Barak was exhibiting the wisdom of God. He recognized Deborah's strengths and godly insight, and he had enough sense to know he would need her continued help in the battle. As it turned out, Deborah became a constant source of counsel to Barak and an invaluable aid in Israel's victory.[12]

This great example of male and female working together to accomplish the purposes of God would not have occurred if Deborah had not lived in the "high place" of the Lord, with her thoughts on God. If she had been self-centered or had allowed any romantic inclinations to interfere with her judgments and actions, this alliance would not have resulted in a victory for the people of God. The prophecy, battle and victory became possible because of Deborah's dedication to the Lord and her life of holiness.

You, too, have a high calling of God on your life. Jesus Christ made a way for you to enter into that high calling, whether you are married or single. Seek God's direction to use your female influence to achieve great victories for Him. Discernment is necessary to avoid romantic traps. Your power of influence already abides within you. You may exercise influence internally through prayer, or externally through your pastor, employer, employees, friends or a class of children.

Shelly is a great example of a single woman who put it all together. She was a bright young woman who completed college and returned to her home church to start her career. Well bred, well groomed and now well educated, she was a great catch for any qualified bachelor. Tongues began to wag, however, when she wouldn't attend the singles class or take part in any of their functions, preferring instead to start a children's band and chorus. Under Shelly's direction the children performed musical plays that brought droves of people into the church and received great reviews from the local press. Year after year Shelly dismissed idle gossip and resolutely stood her ground, insisting that she would not look for a husband, but would do what God called her to do. This response could sound pretty idealistic, but Shelly's commitment to the Lord was rewarded.

A single military officer with an equally deep commitment to the Lord received orders that stationed him near Shelly's town. He wandered for several weeks through various churches and finally asked God specifically what He wanted him to do. The Lord revealed to him that he was to work with children and that he would be divinely lead to the right church. Shelly's pastor saw the "handwriting on the wall" when, in the middle of the week, the handsome bachelor marched into his office saying that he was called to that church to work with children. The pastor gave him Shelly's name and told him simply to show up Sunday morning. Tongues that once wagged now fell limp in gaping mouths as their owners incredulously watched this tall, strapping officer walk right into Shelly's life, just as she had prayed. In a short while Shelly was engaged, then married.

This could not have happened in Shelly's life if she had not stayed in the Word and followed the Lord's leading. Like Deborah, she fastened her thoughts on and put her trust in God, and, also like Deborah, she was rewarded for her faithfulness.

If you are single and desire to be married, there is no better place for you to be than right where you are as you go about your Father's business. If you are single but do not desire to be married, you have placed yourself in position to be of full service to the Father. You will be greatly rewarded for doing so. Either way, keep your eyes on Christ and you will succeed!

- Not only does He provide help and care, God has also promised to be "a father to the fatherless," and the husband of the single woman.

- God can and does reach our children when we ask Him to do so and then step aside and give Him room to work.

- Children will learn to forgive their parents and see the good in them when the parents model and actively teach a positive attitude.

- A healthy, fruitful life is available to *every* single woman by serving the Lord wholeheartedly.

- Whatever your state, you have permission and provision from the Father to be productive, content and complete.

- Every stage of life holds advantages and disadvantages. Use your time! Use your silence! Use your opportunity for productivity and growth!

- You have a high calling of God on your life. Jesus Christ made a way for you to enter into that high calling, whether you are married or single.

Chapter 11

Above Reproach and Beyond It

Down through the years there have been some ridiculous ideas concerning women. Ancient philosophers greatly influenced mankind's interpretation of the Bible and accentuated the sense of reproach held toward women. Much of this anti-female attitude derived from men who didn't know how to control their own passions and blamed them on the woman. Men rationalized that *they* couldn't be at fault, so *women* must be evil. The woman's bondage and reproach increased as these attitudes were reformulated in each succeeding generation.

The state of Pennsylvania once adopted a resolution that stated, "That all women . . . that shall . . . seduce, and betray into matrimony . . . by scents, paints, cosmetic washes, artificial teeth, false hair, Spanish wool, iron stays, hoops, high heeled shoes, [or] bolstered hips [who needs that anyway!], shall incur the penalty of the law in force against witchcraft . . . and that the marriage, upon conviction, shall stand null and void."[1] That we women should be considered witches for trying to look nice is a reproach on our femininity. But what a statement on the power of our influence, that someone would try to outlaw it!

Growing up, I remember a certain adult in my life who often repeated a statement of reproach: "Woman was made

155

for one purpose, for a man's pleasure [i.e., his lust]." I wish I could correct him today with: "Woman was made for the purpose of pleasing God and being a helper to man." Within that statement is the freedom for women to do all that God created us to do with the bonus of a clear conscience and His blessing.

In God there is no lust, no desire to exploit, shame or belittle us. Instead, we please God when by faith we fulfill our potential, rise to greatness and draw close to Him in intimate relationship in which there is no selfishness on either part. Any philosophy of woman apart from God's view of her is a reproach or a source of shame and disgrace.

There are many reproaches against us women. We are reproached with sexual molestation, wife battering and emotional abuse, to name a few. One author stated that psychological abuse was often the most damaging of these reproaches because it is the hardest to pinpoint, and because others around are often unaware of it even in its presence.[2]

We often wonder if we are just imagining the reproach or if we are overly sensitive. And we go about feeling as if the reproach inflicted on us is our own fault or problem. A woman named Amy in one of my Bible classes always looked as though there was a cloud over her. She was a wonderful Christian woman, well-loved and respected, but somehow she always seemed sad. I began to pray specifically for her and asked the Lord to show me a way to help her. One day as I persevered in prayer, the Lord impressed a Scripture on my mind to share with Amy. When the time was right and I approached her about her condition, I found that she had endured a lot of rejection in her life which had resulted in the heaviness of her countenance. I shared the Scripture and prayed with her. When we finished, she said she felt as if a load had been literally lifted off her shoulders and chest. Over a period of time, Amy's countenance changed and developed into the peaceful, serene expression of a saint of God.

A feeling of heaviness and self-pity is often a result of reproach. The psalmist testified to this truth when he wrote, "Reproach hath broken my heart; and I am full of heaviness: and I looked for some to take pity, but there was none; and for comforters, but I found none."[3]

Jesus said that if we continue in His Word, then we will be His disciples and, as His disciples, we will know the truth which will set us free.[4] Knowing and applying the truth sets us free from the effects of reproach.

When you discover God's truth, you can experience the same freedom as Amy. There is no question as to whether you have experienced reproach, for we all have, men and women alike. It is what we do with the reproach that matters in our lives. Rejection was Amy's reproach resulting in heaviness. Another symptom of reproach can be grief that comes from a sense of loss; or rejection that breeds resentment; or anger and strife that produce violence, jealousy and murder (whether verbal or physical). These are fruits of the tree of reproach which must be weeded out or withered from the roots up.

Going head-to-head against the causes of reproach can be rather intimidating. It is the very challenge David dealt with when facing Goliath, the giant who scoffed at the armies of God. "What shall be done to the man that killeth this Philistine, and taketh away the reproach from Israel?" David asked. "For who is this uncircumcised Philistine, that he should defy the armies of the living God?"[5]

The Hebrew word translated "reproach" that David used also means "disgrace," "rebuke," or "shame."[6] In this story David symbolizes Jesus, Who took our reproach on Himself at the Cross to deliver us from its bondage. After uttering those famous words, David stepped forward and, with a sling and stone, killed the giant Goliath. Jesus accomplished just such a victory for us against everything that would bring reproach on us when He defeated Satan at Calvary.

In Proverbs 31 we read about the "virtuous woman." The Hebrew word translated "virtuous" in this passage can also mean "strength," "wealth," and "army."[7] When Peter said to add "courage" to our faith, he used the word "virtue."[8] The virtuous woman is similar to and carries power like a strong, courageous army. In David's story, Goliath defied the armies of God, treating them with disrespect, as unworthy of notice. How many times have we experienced this same type of reproach where someone has treated our womanhood disrespectfully? Both in my personal life and in my ministry there are people who treat me as unworthy of notice. If I accept their view of me and my position, I accept their defeat of me through reproach.

The world has labeled those who bring such reproach "misogynists," "male chauvinists," "anti-feminists," among other names, and proffered seemingly logical steps to overcome that reproach, including civil disobedience, name-calling and out-and-out rebellion. Looking scripturally, however, we see a correct way to counter reproach. Just as David defeated Goliath and liberated the armies of Israel, so Christ defeated Satan and liberated us from reproach. When faced with reproach, we cannot allow ourselves to be intimidated by the size of the giant or the intensity and scope of the jeering, scoffing attitude manifested towards us. Instead, we must look to Jesus Who has already won this battle for us, lay all the reproach on Him, and accept the victory of His Cross.

Reproach can come in many forms but always originates from Satan. Satan hates women. His reproach against us started in the Garden of Eden when man (mankind) first sinned. At that time all of humanity was disconnected from God's grace, which brought reproach or shame upon us all. Remember that besides the shame brought upon mankind, God said that thenceforth there would be a special hatred and hostility between the woman and the serpent, Satan.[9] Satan is called "the prince of the power of the air."[10] He likes to occupy the spiritual realm around us. Because the woman acts as a governor over the unseen world in which Satan wants to reign, it is natural for him to want to bring reproach upon her. If he can shame the woman into being unnoticed or disregarded, then she will no longer be a threat to his domain. This is much the same way in which psychological warfare operates. If someone deflates a person in her heart — for example, a hostage who is made to believe that her country does not care about her, or a battered wife who is conditioned to believe that she deserves whatever she gets — then that individual is no longer a threat because the life has been taken out of her. But the good news is that Jesus has provided a way out of Satan's grasp.

Jesus came and took the consequences of our sin on Himself. At that point, we were freed from the reproach brought on mankind by its sinning against the Old Testament law, and woman was freed from Satan's yoke of shame. When Jesus comes into a woman's life, the yoke of guilt, shame and reproach that Satan has tried to place upon her is utterly and completely lifted.

In our generation, a spiritual veil has drawn back to

expose many hidden abuses people have suffered. Although it is terrible what human beings have endured through the ages, we find hope in the Scripture that states, "Where sin abounded, grace did much more abound."[11] God's Word assures us that where mother and father have let us down (and we can add "husband," "boyfriend" or "friend" without corrupting God's intention), the Lord will be there to lift us up.[12]

God's Word is able to bring both blessing and cursing. We can receive the Word, and the blessing that comes with it, or we can reject the Word, and bring even greater reproach upon ourselves.[13] When we accept Jesus Christ as our Lord and Savior, the Bible says that our old abused selves die, and we are reborn as new creatures.[14] This is what it means to be "born again."[15] Now, as we walk with Jesus daily, He will deliver us and heal us from the effects of that old life — including any reproach and shame that are still attached to us.

The sacrifice of Christ on the Cross provides for total healing and recovery: "Surely he hath borne our griefs, and carried our sorrows," so we don't have to carry them within ourselves any longer. "He was wounded for our transgressions, he was bruised for our iniquities: the chastisement of our peace was upon him; and with his stripes we are healed."[16] As we yield our lives to Him in humble submission, God and His Word will do the healing work within us.

The Lord once revealed to me a specific "shame" that I used to carry. When I was growing up I never knew my father. He was there, and was a good provider, but we never had a conversation that I can recall, much less a relationship. As I mentioned, he died young. I never realized the void this situation created in my life until I became a

Christian and tried to relate to God as a heavenly Father. I certainly didn't know how to be a daughter. Every once in a while I would get depressed and throw myself a real good "pity party," just as the psalmist did who looked for comforters for his reproach but found none.[17]

Then, on a muggy Houston day, I went to a ladies' meeting. The speaker taught about "Jesus the author and finisher of our faith; who for the joy that was set before him endured the cross, *despising the shame*, and is set down at the right hand of the throne of God."[18] The speaker elaborated about the shame of the past that we all deal with and the sense in which we "despise" it, meaning to "think against" it.

I suddenly thought of the shame of not knowing my father. I had never thought of this as "shame," but rather as something I was cheated out of having by some cruel twist of fate. I leaned forward to pay closer attention to the speaker, and realized that although I didn't experience God's best during my early years, Jesus made up for it at Calvary. My childhood left me without knowing how to have a personal relationship with God, but I needn't worry about the lack because Jesus paved the way to God for me. I realized that my focus had been on what I *didn't have* in the past, which I would think *about*, but without understanding. Now I realized this was a shame to me and I needed to think *against* it in order to train my focus on the Cross and what Jesus had *provided for me*, which was a glory for me.

While the meeting went on, I softly repented to the Lord for actually "defying" Him by putting more emphasis on the past than on His provision through Jesus Christ's supreme sacrifice. I made a decision that from that moment forward, whenever I spoke of my father, I would not speak with the negative bitterness that had gripped me for so many years, but would give only the testimony of God's marvelous provision to make me His daughter.

Not too long after that incident I had a tremendous time alone with God in my quiet hour. As I prayed, I realized that my life was being transformed by the Word of God. This revelation experience changed my thinking and produced a great sense of security within me. At that point I knew that God was my true Father and that I was really His daughter.

I had let go of the shame of my past and by an act of my will accepted God as my real Father — and that, I believe, is the key to overcoming shame.

When the Lord Jesus died and forgave us our sins, at that point God began to lavish His favor upon us.[19] Lavish His favor! If we ignore this part of God's Word, we miss out on much of the best of life. We continue with the reproach we have suffered, continue in shame, and never realize that God is waiting for us to let go of the past so He can lavish His favor upon us. There is not room to accept both the blessing and the curse together. We accept one or the other. To accept God's blessings, we have to release the reproach.

Others may have been our source of reproach, or we may have brought it upon ourselves. Regardless of whose fault it is, blaming others will not make us free. Even if we get everyone around us to agree with us in placing the blame, we are still in bondage. To experience freedom we must put our confidence in the blood of Jesus and accept His provision to heal us. Jesus' death and resurrection freed us from distress, released us from blame and guilt, and repaired and restored us.

Once set at liberty, to continue to live freely we must change our habits of thought. This comes by repeatedly hearing, reading and speaking the Word of God and points to the importance of daily devotions, regular church attendance and Christian friendships.

The story of Samson and Delilah in the Bible is full of symbolism about reproach. If we build on the word meanings, we see how our lives can parallel Samson's, and his mistakes can be our lessons. In the story, Samson was born under miraculous circumstances, named for "sunlight"[20] and nurtured to be a mighty man of God. He grew in strength and power until he was considered the strongest man alive, which threatened his enemies, the Philistines. In his early manhood, he went to Gaza and saw a harlot with whom he began a relationship.[21] Her name was Delilah, which means "languishing," "*feeble*," "*oppressed*," or "dried up."[22]

The Philistines conspired with Delilah to discover what made Samson so strong. She seduced Samson, who was quite a willing victim. The more time he spent with her, the more of his heart he shared with her. In the intimacy of their relationship, Samson finally told her the source of his strength, the Nazarite vow he kept from birth that he expressed by never cutting his hair. Immediately she called his enemies who captured him, cut his hair to drain his strength, then gouged out his eyes to put him forever at their mercy.

Here was a man with seeds of greatness who took up with a harlot who, true to her name, became oppressive to him and dried him up. Like Samson and his miraculous birth, through the miracle of "new birth" we become the "light of the world,"[23] children of the living God,[24] with His seed planted within us to make us great.[25] The Apostle Paul said, "Prove yourselves to be blameless and innocent, children of God *above reproach* in the midst of a crooked and perverse generation, among whom you appear as *lights in the world*, holding fast the word of life."[26]

Even with all this going for us — being free from reproach, being children of light and having the word of life within us — we can still be deluged with oppressive thoughts and memories. Because our flesh feeds on the negative and pitiable, sometimes we cling to such thoughts, causing us to forget the promises of God. Many people use oppressive memories to manipulate others to like them or feel sorry for them. This is like a child playing with a loaded gun. Emotionally and mentally dwelling on and "abiding" with negative, evil, oppressive thoughts and memories results in harm because they are literally the enemy's weapon.

Samson's long hair symbolizes God's covering of glory that comes from keeping covenant with Him. When we were born again, Jesus took our old covering of sin and replaced it with His "coat of righteousness"[27] to make us new creatures and give us His strength. Like Samson, becoming intimate with oppressive thoughts and memories that are far from God's promises separates us from the glory of God and drains our strength.

The Apostle Paul cautioned us to keep our minds on that which is pure, holy and of a good report.[28] What we think on long enough will eventually affect our spirit and color our perceptions: "As he [a person] thinketh in his heart, so is he."[29]

By abiding with oppression, Samson lost his strength, then his sight. The Bible says, "Where there is no vision, the people perish."[30] People who are bent on believing negative thoughts, who dwell continually on oppressive memories, lose their vision of what God has done for them and what He will do for them. Their focus is not on Christ's provision, but on the reproach of the oppressor.

In order to enjoy God's lavish favor we must believe on Jesus, and then resist the "Delilah" images that stray into our minds. Our enemy, the devil, will try to get us to dwell on evil thoughts about ourselves and those around us. We do one little thing wrong and instantly Satan is there with, "Ha! And you call yourself a Christian!" How many times have you heard that one? Don't believe it! Look to Jesus and His estimation of you now that you have received Him. You are not condemned — you stand forgiven! If you fall, ask God's forgiveness and go on in His favor.

If we will resist the devil, purposely think on what the Lord says about us and our situation, and then speak out His promises, God will move on our behalf to prove that His Word is true. Right, truthful thinking becomes an avenue of power for us.

To complete our story, Samson ultimately died a hero. Through His grace, the Lord removed Samson's reproach. While in captivity, Samson's captors brought him out for entertainment at their parties and ridiculed him, never noticing that his hair was growing out. On one of these occasions, Samson had someone put his hands on the pillars of the great house and he cried out to God, "Let me die with the Philistines." He pushed against the pillars, which collapsed the arena, killing more Philistines in his death than he had while he was alive.[31]

The Scriptures I read when Amy was freed from heaviness were "Reproach hath broken my heart; and I am full of heaviness,"[32] and "to give unto them beauty for ashes, the oil of joy for mourning, the garment of praise for the spirit of heaviness."[33]

Praise is the antidote to the spirit of heaviness that comes from reproach. Praise is one of our greatest avenues of power to bring God's glory into a given situation. God inhabits the praises of His people.[34] Praising the Lord releases us to another avenue of power — faith. Amy accepted these words from God and by faith threw off the straightjacket of reproach, receiving Christ's provision to usher her into new life and God's favor.

What a glorious healing word from God!

There is a caution in Scripture. Refusing to receive God's Word and Christ's provision of freedom from reproach can result in falling away from Him: "Take care, brethren, lest there should be in any one of you an evil, unbelieving heart, in falling away from the living God."[35] An evil heart is a heart full of hurt or "disease." How important it is to God that we believe on His Word, and accept who His Word says we are in Christ.

You can do the same thing with your shame that Amy did with hers and I did with mine. Repent before God for holding on to the reproach and denying God's favor. Determine to stop looking back and start looking at Jesus. Commit to receive God's grace even though you may not feel anything at first. He will commit to you, and your healing process will begin. Our God is looking for women who dare to believe His Word!

How often we diminish God's glory by focusing on the negative instead of on the victorious Cross of Christ. Every moment holds glory for us because of all the Lord has provided for us through His Son Jesus. What looked like a defeat at the Cross was mankind's greatest triumph. Death is swallowed up in victory.[36] What looks like defeat to you today is the occasion for God's greatest triumph in your life as well.

Samson was more effective at his death than he was in his life. Jesus was most effective at His death and resurrection, which made it possible for the entire world to come to God through Him. Likewise, we are more effective in our death when we let go of the old self, the past shame, and become alive, "born again" as a new creature: "Unless a grain of wheat falls into the earth and dies, it remains by itself alone; but if it dies, it bears much fruit."[37]

Plant the seed of your life today. Make a decision to live up to God's purpose for your life and hold fast to your position. Learn the avenues of power available to you to achieve God's will, which is your highest good. Let the old way you thought and lived die so that out of your life springs fruit, success, power, achievement and fulfillment.

Where do you go from here? Following is a short prayer you can pray. Even when we are seasoned Christian women, it is always good to renew our commitment to the Lord. As you choose to go His way, may He bless you and yours and fulfill His every desire for goodness in and through you by the power of His Spirit.

"Father, I desire to be a woman of Your Word. I am asking You to forgive me for my sins, forgive me for wherever I have missed the mark of Your glory. Thank You for Jesus Christ, His shed blood and the forgiveness of my sins. I ask Jesus into my life to change me and bring me into Your purposes and Your power. I want Your will to be accomplished in and through me. Thank You, Lord. Amen."

- By pleasing God and helping man, we women have the freedom to do all God created us to do with the bonus of a clear conscience and His blessing.

- We please God when by faith we fulfill our potential, rise to greatness and draw close to Him in intimate relationship in which there is no selfishness on either part.

- Where your focus is on the past, which is a shame to you, you need to train your focus on the Cross and what Jesus provided, which is a glory to you.

- Let go of the shame of your past and by an act of your will accept God as your real Father.

- God is waiting for us to let go of the past so He can lavish His favor upon us.

- Whether or not we caused the shame to come on ourselves, we can still be free from it.

- What we think on long enough will eventually affect our spirit and color our perceptions.

- Determine to stop looking back and start looking at Jesus.

- God is looking for women who dare to believe His Word!

- Every moment holds glory for us because of all God has done for us through His Son Jesus.

Endnotes

Chapter 1

[1] Psalm 139:15,16 NIV

[2] Ronald W. Clark, *Einstein: The Life and Times* (New York: Avon Books, 1971), p. 97

[3] Acts 10:34

[4] John 12:24; 1 Corinthians 15:36

[5] 1 Thessalonians 5:23

[6] Matthew 7:13,14; Proverbs 2:1-6; Matthew 7:7,8

[7] Hebrews 11:3

[8] John 3:3

[9] Ezekiel 28:11-19; see also *The New Laymen's Bible Commentary* (Grand Rapids: Zondervan Publishing House, 1979), p. 886

[10] 2 Corinthians 4:4; Colossians 1:13

[11] Matthew 13:41; 2 Thessalonians 2:7 AMP; James 3:14-16

[12] Proverbs 27:20; Ecclesiastes 1:8; Romans 3:23

[13] John 8:12

[14] John 3:16; Ephesians 1:6

[15] John 14:21

[16] Matthew 5:14; John 1:9; 6:40; Ephesians 5:8

[17] James Strong, *Strong's Exhaustive Concordance* (Iowa Falls, IA: World Bible Publishers, n.d.), Greek Dictionary, p. 77, entry #5485

[18] 1 Corinthians 13:5 NAS

[19] 1 Corinthians 13:8 NAS

[20] Deuteronomy 30:19 NIV

[21] John 3:3

[22] John 3:5; 9:25; see also John Newton, "Amazing Grace," stanza 1

[23] Romans 10:10

Chapter 2

[1] Genesis 1:27 NAS

[2] Genesis 2:18

[3] Psalm 30:10; 54:4

[4] John 14:16 NAS

[5] John 14:16 AMP

6 Galatians 3:28

7 Proverbs 10:12; 1 Peter 4:8

8 Nehemiah 1

9 2 Corinthians 1:3,4

10 Matthew Henry, *An Exposition of the Old and New Testament* (London: Frederick Westley & A. H. Davis, 1836), Vol. i, Note 1, p. 12

11 Psalm 103:4 NAS

12 Strong, Hebrew Dictionary, p. 87, entries #5849-5850

13 Psalm 5:12

14 Ezekiel 22:30 NAS

15 "Coach," CBS Television, March 10, 1993

16 Ephesians 2:10

17 Genesis 2:21

18 *New American Standard Bible* (Philadelphia: A.J. Holman, Co., n.d.), footnote to Genesis 2:18, p. 3

19 Q. M. Adams, *Neither Male Nor Female* (Dallas: Christ for the Nations, 1973, 1977, 1984), p. 20

20 C. J. Ellicott, *An Old Testament Commentary* (London: Cassell & Company, 1884), Vol. i, p. 22

21 1 Peter 3:4

22 Hebrews 2:1

23 Luke 10:38-40

24 Genesis 2:22-25

25 1 Timothy 2:12

26 Strong, Greek Dictionary, p. 17, entry #831

27 Genesis 2:9; 3:6

28 Proverbs 4:23; James 1:14,15

29 Isaiah 54:5

30 Psalm 68:5

31 John 14:16; 16:13-15

32 John 15:12-14

33 John 16:27; Philippians 4:19

Chapter 3

1 1 Corinthians 11:12

2 1 Corinthians 11:3

3 Strong, Greek Dictionary, p. 22, entry #1223

4 1 Peter 3:1-7

5 1 Peter 3:1,2

[6] 1 Corinthians 13:8 NKJV

[7] Ephesians 5:33 AMP

[8] Ephesians 5:25

[9] Quote from Edwin Louis Cole

[10] To take the point even further, God Himself divides His powers in much the same way we see the powers of male and female divided. "But to us there is but one God, the Father, of whom are all things . . . and one Lord Jesus Christ, by whom are all things" (1 Cor. 8:6). As all things are *of* God, and all things are *by* Jesus, this passage mirrors 1 Corinthians 11:12 which states that the woman is *of* the man, and the man is *by* the woman. In this passage, God the Father expresses the male from Whom and for Whose purposes all things originate, and Jesus the Son expresses the female by Whom, or through Whom, all things develop. A similar passage is, "All things were created by him, and for him" (Col. 1:16) — "by him" meaning developing from Him, and "for him" meaning originating for His purposes. On earth, Jesus Christ came to show us the full expression of the Father, so He fulfilled both male and female functions in His human life. We can see that in relation to the Father, Jesus is in the role of submission, which a woman would fill in relation to a husband. In relation to the Church, Jesus is in the male role of authority. (Col. 1:18.) We will see more about these roles when we discuss our position as women.

[11] Karen S. Petersen, "Debate: Does 'Wiring' rule emotion, skill?" *USA TODAY*, Jul. 8, 1992, p. 1A

[12] Donald M. Joy, Ph.D., *Bonding Relationships in the Image of God* (Waco: Word Books, 1985), pp. 89,90

[13] 1 Corinthians 11:11,12

[14] Joy, p. 92

[15] Focus on the Family interview with Dr. Donald Joy, n.d.

[16] Christine Gorman, "Sizing Up the Sexes," *TIME*, Jan. 20, 1992, p. 44

[17] Ibid.

[18] Margaret Mitchell, *Gone With the Wind* (New York: MacMillan Publishing Company, 1936, 1964), p. 1031

[19] Psalm 107:20

[20] Gorman, pp. 42,44

[21] Genesis 1:26,27; 2 Corinthians 6:1

[22] Edwin Louis Cole, *Maximized Manhood* (Springdale, PA: Whitaker House, 1982), p. 147

[23] James 1:5-7

Chapter 4

[1] John 1:1-12; Mark 2:10; 1 John 1:9

[2] Exodus 38:8; in the Old Testament God revealed Himself through the lives, adventures, failings and successes of His people. Whereas the New Testament is like a textbook, speaking directly to us about specific areas of our lives, the Old Testament is like a picture story book in which we learn by symbol and example. The Old Testament story of the Hebrew children journeying to their Promised Land from slavery in Egypt and building a Tabernacle along the way, is actually a pattern of heavenly things. (Heb. 8:5.) The Tabernacle represents the place where God dwells, which is now within us since Jesus died, was resurrected, ascended into heaven, and sent His Spirit to dwell within those of us who believe. (1 Cor. 6:19.) Because we are the new Tabernacle, the original building relates to our lives. The original Tabernacle contained three sections. To enter the first, one would pass through a gate and come to a bronze altar on which the priests placed the sacrificial lamb (the lamb whose place Jesus took). After the altar one would come to the laver. The laver was a large basin set on a pedestal and filled with water in which the priests washed their hands and feet before entering the next section of the Tabernacle, a covered area called the Holy Place. Within the Holy Place a curtain separated an even smaller chamber, the Holy of Holies, into which only the high priest could enter once a year. The Holy of Holies was the place wherein God's presence settled.

[3] Ibid.

[4] Taken from the feminine form of a Hebrew word meaning "view"; Strong, Hebrew Dictionary, p. 72, entries #4758-4759

[5] 1 Peter 3:1-3

[6] 1 Peter 3:1-3

[7] Compare this thought to that of Ephesians 5:27 which tells us that Jesus Christ will present to Himself a Church free of "spot, or wrinkle, or any such thing." Ephesians 5:26 notes that He will sanctify His Church and "cleanse it with the washing of water by the word." Like the laver of the Tabernacle which held the holy water, women who hold the Word of God in their spirits are used by God as a cleansing element to sanctify His Church. In no way does this relieve the man of his responsibilities in the home or church, nor does it discount the fact that he can

exercise influence and serve as a cleansing element. We are speaking to women from the woman's perspective. Our purpose is not to "let men off the hook," but to strengthen women in their purpose and power.

[8] Genesis 1:16

[9] Genesis 37:8-10

[10] Psalm 19

[11] 1 Corinthians 11:7

[12] James Kennedy, *Why I Believe* (Dallas: Word Publishing, 1980), p. 42

[13] 1 Peter 3:3,4

[14] James 1:14

[15] In Proverbs 7:10, which speaks of the harlot and her attire and nature, the meaning of the expression "subtil of heart" used in regard to her means simply that she guards or conceals her heart; Strong, Hebrew Dictionary, p. 80, entry #5341

[16] Proverbs 30:20 NIV

[17] Genesis 2:24

[18] Quote from Marie Powers of Seattle who lectures on women's issues. A set of seven tapes is available from her at the following address and phone: 1823-207 Pl. SW, Lynnwood, Washington (206) 778-7070.

[19] 1 Peter 3:6

Chapter 5

[1] Proverbs 31:10; in this verse the Hebrew word translated "virtuous" can also mean "*force*...an *army, wealth, virtue, valor, strength*," Strong, Hebrew Dictionary, p. 39, entry #2428

[2] Proverbs 3:13-15

[3] Proverbs 3:13 NAS

[4] Proverbs 8:35 NAS

[5] Proverbs 18:22 NAS

[6] 1 Peter 3:7

[7] Proverbs 4:5-9

[8] Ephesians 5:33 AMP

[9] Proverbs 1:7

[10] Proverbs 31:11,12; Strong, Hebrew Dictionary, p. 20, entry #982

[11] Matthew 18:19

[12] Proverbs 19:14

[13] Strong, Hebrew Dictionary, p. 116, entry #7919; *Webster's New World Dictionary* (Cleveland: The World Publishing Company, 1957), s.v. "circumspect"

[14] Proverbs 18:22
[15] Proverbs 8:22-31
[16] Proverbs 15:2
[17] Proverbs 15:7

Chapter 6
[1] 1 Corinthians 14:33
[2] John 15:16 AMP
[3] Genesis 3:15 NAS
[4] 2 Chronicles 20:17 NKJV
[5] 1 Corinthians 11:3; although not related to the chapter under discussion, here are some of my thoughts on the rest of that passage:

> "But I would have you know, that the head of every man is Christ; and the head of the woman is the man; and the head of Christ is God. . . . For this cause ought the woman to have power on her head because of the angels."
>
> 1 Corinthians 11:3,10

Theologians have wrestled with this reference to angels for years. Although many interpretations may lend themselves to controversy, I would like to present one application with which most would agree. Angels are given to us as ministering spirits. (Heb. 1:14.) They are sent to serve us when we receive Jesus Christ as our Savior; they also help us to be overcomers. Some angels left their rightful positions in the Kingdom of God, but our ministering angels obey the Lord and His Word spoken by His servants in faith. (Ps. 103:20.) Satan's kingdom is made up of disobedient angels who rebelled against God and did as they pleased. From their example, we can learn how important it is to stay in position and obey the Word of God. So, the part of this passage that states that the woman ought to have "power on her head because of the angels" can mean that we should follow their example in submitting to the will of God. It illustrates that angels cannot serve us in their full purpose when we are out of place. In the last days, angels will play an even greater part in what God is doing:

> "The Son of man shall send forth his angels, and they shall gather out of his kingdom all things that offend, and them which do iniquity."
>
> Matthew 13:41

Angels will be used to gather up those who do iniquity, which means those who are lawless or rebellious against constituted authority. (2 Thessalonians 2:7 AMP.) They will be cast out of God's Kingdom eternally. As women of God, we want to maintain our good standing with God through Christ and not have anything to do with such iniquity.

[6] Psalm 84:11
[7] 1 Samuel 25:3
[8] 1 Samuel 25:17
[9] 1 Samuel 25:24-31
[10] 2 Peter 3:9
[11] 2 Peter 3:9
[12] Quoted from personal appearances of Edwin Louis Cole
[13] 2 Corinthians 4:10-12
[14] 2 Corinthians 10:6
[15] Romans 12:21
[16] John 1:5 AMP
[17] 1 Corinthians 15:54; 2 Corinthians 5:4

Chapter 7
[1] Greeting card (Oakland, NJ: Russ Berrie and Company, Inc., 1991)
[2] 1 Timothy 2:1,2
[3] Strong, Greek Dictionary, p. 12, entry #444
[4] Exodus 15:20; Micah 6:4
[5] Judges 4:4,5
[6] 2 Kings 22:14
[7] Romans 16:1
[8] 1 Corinthians 11:3
[9] John Temple Bristow, *What Paul Really Said About Women* (San Francisco: Harper & Row, 1988), pp. 36,37
[10] Strong, Greek Dictionary, p. 42, entry #2776
[11] 1 Peter 3:5
[12] Ephesians 5:21,22,24 RSV (emphasis added)
[13] Bristow, p. 40
[14] Bristow, pp. 40,41; another definition carries a military sense, meaning to take a position in an army (Bristow, p. 41). In line with this attitude of military order, the Bible says to worship the Lord in "holy array" (1 Chron. 16:29 NAS). "Array" means military order. It can also mean honor, attire and adornment. When we operate from our orderly position, we are truly worshipping God by taking on the covering He provides for us with our rightful authorities. Again, what most often gets

in the way of our submission to rightful authority and to one another is the pride of life.

[15] Rick Atkinson, *The Long Gray Line* (New York: Pocket Star Books, 1989), pp. 574,575
[16] 2 Corinthians 6:17
[17] 1 Peter 3:18
[18] James 4:7
[19] 2 Corinthians 12:9
[20] Strong, Greek Dictionary, p. 24, entry #1411
[21] Strong, Greek Dictionary, p. 71, entry #5048
[22] Strong, Greek Dictionary, p. 16, entry #769
[23] Philippians 3:10 NKJV
[24] 1 John 2:16
[25] Jeremiah 33:3
[26] James 3:16
[27] 1 Peter 3:6
[28] Strong, Greek Dictionary, p. 62, entries #4423, 4422
[29] 1 Peter 3:4
[30] Colossians 3:18,19
[31] Colossians 3:18 NKJV
[32] Romans 14:23 NKJV
[33] Matthew 8:9
[34] Matthew 8:10
[35] Proverbs 15:23
[36] 1 Samuel 15:22
[37] Hebrews 10:7

Chapter 8
[1] Titus 2:3,4 NKJV, KJV
[2] Titus 2:5 NAS
[3] Proverbs 4:23
[4] Exodus 20:12 NKJV
[5] Deuteronomy 21:18-21
[6] 1 John 1:7
[7] Matthew 18:18; 28:18-20
[8] Mark 16:20; John 1:1-3
[9] 2 Corinthians 10:4; Ephesians 6:13-17
[10] Galatians 3:28
[11] Proverbs 31:15

[12] Proverbs 31:21,22
[13] Psalm 139:11,12
[14] Ruth 1:16,17
[15] 1 Samuel 25:23-25
[16] Esther 2:7,17
[17] Ephesians 3:20

Chapter 9

[1] Matthew 16:26
[2] Matthew 6:13
[3] Strong, Greek Dictionary, p. 59, entry #4190; *Thayers Greek-English Lexicon of the New Testament* (Grand Rapids: Baker Book House, 1977), p. 530
[4] Focus on the Family bulletin, September 1992
[5] 1 Corinthians 1:30
[6] Galatians 2:20

Chapter 10

[1] James 1:27 KJV and AMP
[2] Psalm 68:5,6; Isaiah 54:5
[3] Genesis 3:16
[4] Philippians 4:11; 1 Timothy 6:6
[5] 1 Corinthians 7:34
[6] Colossians 2:9,10 (emphasis added)
[7] 1 Corinthians 7:8
[8] The Bible describes Deborah as a woman who "dwelt under the palm tree . . . between Ramah and Bethel" (Judges 4:5). The palm tree is a poetic symbol of upright stature, justice and righteousness. It also symbolizes holiness and resurrection in Christian worship (Michael Zoharty, *Plants of the Bible* (New York: Cambridge University Press, 1982), p. 60). The names of the two cities on either side of her mean "high place" (Strong, Hebrew Dictionary, p. 109, entry #7414) and "house of God" (Strong, Hebrew Dictionary, p. 20, entry #1008). If we take the symbols and interpret them for our benefit today, we see that Deborah is a woman who lived in upright stature, justice and righteousness. She rested in the resurrection power of God and lived in a high place, or in the house of God.
[9] Judges 4:5
[10] Judges 4:6
[11] Judges 4:8 (paraphrased)

[12] Judges 4:14,23,24

Chapter 11
[1] "Ask Marilyn" column, *Parade* magazine, Nov. 8, 1992, p. 16
[2] Burton Stokes and Lynn Lucas, *No Longer a Victim* (Shippenburg, PA: Destiny Image Publishers, 1988), pp. 135,136
[3] Psalm 69:20
[4] John 8:31,32
[5] 1 Samuel 17:26
[6] Strong, Hebrew Dictionary, p. 44, entry #2781
[7] Strong, Hebrew Dictionary, p. 39, entry #2428
[8] 2 Peter 1:5
[9] Genesis 3:15
[10] Ephesians 2:2
[11] Romans 5:20
[12] Psalm 27:10
[13] The psalmist says that the Lord crowned him with lovingkindness and tender mercies. (Ps. 103:4.) The Hebrew word translated "lovingkindness" in this passage means "*kindness*," "favour" or "mercy," but it also can mean "*reproof*" or "reproach" (Strong, Hebrew Dictionary, p. 41, entry #2617). This is odd unless we realize that God's Word brings a curse or reproach on the one who refuses to believe it, while it brings a blessing to the believer.
[14] 2 Corinthians 5:17
[15] John 3:3,7
[16] Isaiah 53:4,5
[17] Psalm 69:20
[18] Hebrews 12:2 (emphasis added)
[19] Ephesians 1:6-8 NAS
[20] Strong, Hebrew Dictionary, p. 119, entry #8123
[21] Judges 16; a harlot is a woman who gives her body but conceals her heart. (Prov. 7:10.) An adulteress is one who forgets her covenant with God. (Prov. 2:16,17.)
[22] Strong, Hebrew Dictionary, p. 30, entries #1807-1809; Delilah was from the land of Sorek, which symbolically means "a vine . . . the richest variety" (Strong, Hebrew Dictionary, pp. 114, 121, entries #7796, 8321). So Delilah is part of a rich vine of reproach and shame. Jesus gave us another vine to be part of, one that is better by far:

> "I am the vine, you are the branches; he who abides in

Me, and I in him, he bears much fruit; for apart from Me you can do nothing.

"*If anyone does not abide in Me,* he is thrown away as a branch, and *dries up*; and they gather them, and cast them into the fire, and they are burned."

John 15:5,6 NAS

You and I are part of a rich vine, one that releases us from the grip of oppression.

[23] Matthew 5:14
[24] Romans 8:16
[25] 1 Peter 1:23
[26] Philippians 2:15,16 NAS (emphasis added)
[27] 1 Corinthians 1:30
[28] Philippians 4:8
[29] Proverbs 23:7
[30] Proverbs 29:18
[31] Judges 16:30
[32] Psalm 69:20
[33] Isaiah 61:3
[34] Psalm 22:3
[35] Hebrews 3:12 NAS
[36] 1 Corinthians 15:54
[37] John 12:24 NAS

References

Scripture quotations marked AMP are taken from *The Amplified Bible, New Testament*. Copyright © 1958, 1987, by the Lockman Foundation, La Habra, California. Used by permission.

Scripture quotations marked NIV are taken from *The Holy Bible: New International Version*. Copyright © 1973, 1978, 1984 by the International Bible Society. Used by permission of Zondervan Bible Publishers.

Scripture quotations marked RSV are taken from *The Revised Standard Version of the Bible*, copyright © 1946, Old Testament section copyright © 1952 by the Division of Christian Education of the Churches of Christ in the United States of America and is used by permission.

Scripture quotations marked NAS are taken from the *New American Standard Bible*. Copyright © The Lockman Foundation 1960, 1962, 1963, 1968, 1971, 1972, 1973, 1975, 1977. Used by permission.

Scripture quotations marked NKJV are taken from *The New King James Version of the Bible*. Copyright© 1979, 1980, 1982 by Thomas Nelson, Inc., Publishers. Used by permission.

Mary Jean Pidgeon

Mary Jean Pidgeon is a wife, the mother of three grown sons and the founder of "The Restoration of Women's Virtues," a ministry to support and strengthen women. Born and raised in Houston, Texas, she received Jesus as her Savior in March of 1972 and shortly thereafter began to share God's Word through a teaching ministry. She has been active in women's ministries for the last sixteen years through teaching Bible studies and conducting seminars. Mary Jean has a special message concerning the purpose of the woman, which she has shared through radio and television. She now conducts weekly and monthly meetings training women in their original purpose and power for service to the Lord Jesus Christ.

Jack and Mary Jean Pidgeon frequently host the local TBN Praise the Lord television program in their area. They may be reached by writing or calling:

Restoration of Women's Virtues
P. O. Box 440754
Houston, TX 77244-0754

J. C. Webster

Joann Cole Webster — writer, editor, wife and mother of two teenaged sons — is a *summa cum laude* graduate of Southern California College. She has served as a missions assistant for an interdenominational mission group in Japan and presently serves on the Board of Directors of God's House of Prayer, a fifty-year-old church-planting organization. For eighteen years she has worked with her father, Edwin Louis Cole, to establish the International Christian Men's Network and is currently Director of Marketing and Director of Finance.

She has assisted her father in writing his books; such as *Courage, Strong Men in Tough Times* and *Facing the Challenge of Crisis and Change*; and has helped write many other books including *Tapestry of Life* by Nancy Corbett Cole, *It's Who You Know* by Dr. A. R. Bernard, and *The No Direction Generation* by Dr. Doug Stringer.

Additional copies of this book
are available from your local bookstore,
or from:

HARRISON HOUSE
P.O. Box 74153
Tulsa, OK 74153

Additional copies of book
are available
in Canada from:

Word Alive
P.O. Box 670
Niverville, Manitoba
CANADA R0A 1E0

The Harrison House Vision

Proclaiming the truth and the power
Of the Gospel of Jesus Christ
With excellence;

Challenging Christians to
Live victoriously,
Grow Spiritually,
Know God intimately.